# 90 Ways To Get Saucy

with

Dressings, Marinades, Creams and Mousses

for

Salads, Fish, Meat, Poultry & Desserts

by

Elizabeth Tuddenham

*Best Wishes*

*E Tuddenham*

**Published by Kodey Limited**
publications@kodey-limited.co.uk
www.kodey-limited.co.uk

Copyright © Kodey Limited 2014.
Text and illustrations copyright © Elizabeth Tuddenham 2014.

The right of Elizabeth J. Tuddenham to be identified as the author of this work has been asserted by her in accordance with the Copyright, Design and Patents Act, 1988.

All rights reserved. No part of this publication may be reproduced, stored in a retrieval system, or transmitted in any form or by any means, electronic, mechanical, photocopying, recording or otherwise, without the prior written permission from Kodey Limited.

First published in Great Britain in 2014

ISBN: 978-1-910466-00-1

Cover design by Kodey Limited
Illustrations by the author Elizabeth J. Tuddenham
Printed and bound by Short Run Press Limited, shortrunpress.co.uk

## Acknowledgements

I want to thank my family for their encouragement and my son Scott for his help, motivation and technical advice in making this recipe book. It just would not have happened without his support.

Thank you to all my students for their help and ideas and in memory of my mother and great aunt Betty with all their recipes, advice, patience and experience in teaching me so much. I have treasured memories of the large wooden kitchen table being covered with various ingredients.

My thanks to Mark at Short Run Press for his advice, patience and getting this delightful book onto the printing press.

# Contents

of

sauces, dressings, marinades, creams and mousses.

*Each recipe serves 4 to 6 people*

Introduction

Salads
- Calming Rosemary Dressing — 2
- Basil and Balsamic Creamy Dressing — 2
- Herb and Celery Light Dressing — 4
- Herb Salad with Lemon Oil Dressing — 4
- Egg and Sweet Almond Oil Dressing — 6
- Creamy Salad Dressing — 6
- Olive Oil Dressing — 8
- Mother's Salad Cream — 8
- Mustard Mayonnaise Sauce — 10
- Garlic and Sherry Vinegar Dressing — 10
- Homemade Mayonnaise — 12
- Tomato, Basil and Red Onion Side Dressing — 14
- Thyme and Sour Cream Dressing — 14
- Watercress Cream — 16
- Balsamic and Garlic Dressing — 16
- Cashew and Apple Coleslaw Dressing — 18
- Tomato and Yoghurt Dressing — 18
- Rich Cheese and Onion Sauce — 20

Fish
- Freshwater Fish Marinade — 24
- Tarragon and Celery Sauce — 24
- Creamy White Sauce — 26
- Lime and Turmeric Mayonnaise — 26
- Hollandaise Sauce — 28
- Walnut and Herb Marinade — 30
- General Tartar Sauce — 30
- Homemade White Sauce — 32

## Fish *continued*...

| | |
|---|---|
| Tomato and Coriander Sauce | 32 |
| Mustard and Garlic Dressing | 34 |
| Homemade Parsley Sauce | 34 |
| Homemade Mornay Sauce | 36 |
| Mustard and Lemon Sauce | 36 |
| Dressing for Salmon | 38 |
| Avocado Sauce | 38 |
| Herb Butter Sauce | 40 |
| Potato and Wine Sauce | 40 |
| White Wine Cream | 42 |

## Meat

| | |
|---|---|
| Medium Hot Dry Pepper Mix | 46 |
| Fresh Mint Sauce | 46 |
| Tasty Curry and Honey Sauce | 48 |
| Homemade Tomato Sauce | 48 |
| Sweet and Sour Sauce | 50 |
| Apple Sauce | 50 |
| Redcurrant and Ginger Sauce | 52 |
| Mushroom and Yoghurt Sauce | 54 |
| Homemade Horseradish Sauce | 54 |
| Herb Butter | 56 |
| A Simple Tomato Sauce | 56 |
| An Oriental Sauce | 58 |
| Cucumber and Yoghurt Mixture | 60 |
| Cool Tomato Relish | 60 |
| Barbecue Sauce | 62 |
| Cold Cucumber Sauce | 64 |
| Lentil and Bacon Dressing | 64 |
| Yorkshire Pudding Mixture | 66 |
| A Spanish Sauce | 66 |
| Madeira Sauce | 68 |
| Medium White Sauce | 68 |

## Poultry

| | |
|---|---|
| Celery Sauce | 72 |
| Homemade Bread Sauce | 72 |
| Morello Cherry Sauce | 74 |
| Asparagus Sauce | 74 |
| Thyme and Parsley Balls | 76 |

Poultry *continued...*
- Chilli Dipping Sauce — 78
- Creamy Orange Sauce — 78
- Barbecue Chicken Marinade — 80
- Garlic and Chilli Cream — 82
- Cherry Sauce — 82
- Mixed Fruit Sauce — 84
- Sweet Orange Marinade — 84
- Red Wine Sauce — 86
- Mixed Spice and Yoghurt Sauce — 86
- Red Wine Marinade — 88

Desserts
- Creamy Chocolate Sauce — 92
- Amaretto Sauce — 92
- Lemon Sauce — 94
- Brandy Sauce — 94
- Butterscotch Sauce — 96
- Raspberry and Honey Sauce — 96
- Strawberry Sauce — 98
- Chocolate Sauce — 98
- Fresh Vanilla Custard Sauce — 100
- Grand Marnier Cream — 100
- Whipped Brandy Butter — 102
- Granola Topping — 102
- Highland Cream Sauce — 104
- Yoghurt Snow Cream — 104
- Banana Ice Cream — 106
- Apricot Whipped Mousse — 106
- Simple Caramel Sauce — 108
- Macaroon Biscuit Cream — 108

# Introduction

I have always been interested in eating good food and foods that compliment each other. This book is designed to give recipes for sauces, dressings, creams and mousses that are quick and easy to prepare and with ingredients that are likely to be already in your larder.

Changes in life styles and eating habits, poorer knowledge of cooking and concerns about calories and cholesterol have meant that ingredients play a very important factor so all the recipes in this book are with health in mind.

Even if you are not a fan of preparing meals, these recipes not only compliment a meal but make a plain meal more interesting and tasty. A lot of these sauces, dressings, creams and mousses can be made and kept in the fridge for a day or two or in the freezer for a week or so, making less work when preparing for large celebrations or get-togethers with a few friends.

# Helpful Hints

Sometimes curdling can occur with butter and egg based sauces. When this happens use a little stabiliser such as cornflour to help things.

If the sauce has curdled, it can be corrected with egg yolk sauces. The remedy is use a fresh egg yolk and start again by adding the curdled ingredients to it. If making a sauce with egg, butter, vinegar or lemon cornflour will prevent curdling occurring as this is an excellent stabiliser.

# ~ Salads ~

## Calming Rosemary Dressing

**Ingredients:**

1 clove of garlic
2 teaspoon balsamic oil
Two stalks of rosemary (chopped very finely)
2 tablespoons olive oil
A little salt and pepper to taste

**Method:**

Crush or finely chop the garlic, add chopped rosemary. Heat in a pan with the Olive oil for two minutes.

Remove from heat, add the balsamic oil, salt and pepper.

Additionally, you can separately stir-fry onions, courgettes, sunflower seeds, leeks, tomatoes. Then add this to the dressing - delicious!!

Serve with side salad and French bread.


## Basil and Balsamic Creamy Dressing

**Ingredients:**

1 tablespoon olive oil
1 teaspoon yoghurt
four leaves fresh basil (chopped)
1 teaspoon balsamic cream
1 teaspoon Knorr Aromat all purpose savoury seasoning (specifically) add a little milk or more oil to keep consistency creamy.

**Method:**

Put all the ingredients together in a bowl and mix together.

Let it stand in the fridge for five minutes then take out and stir again.

Do not add to the salad until ready to serve or alternatively put into a little dish so everyone can help themselves and pour onto their own salad.

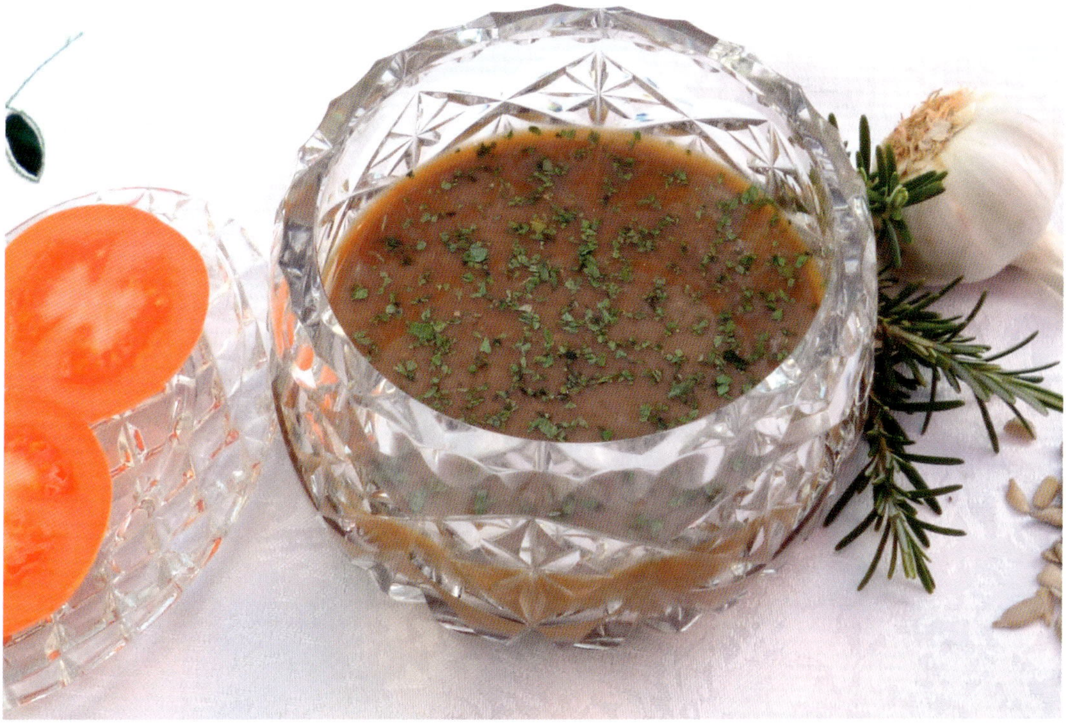

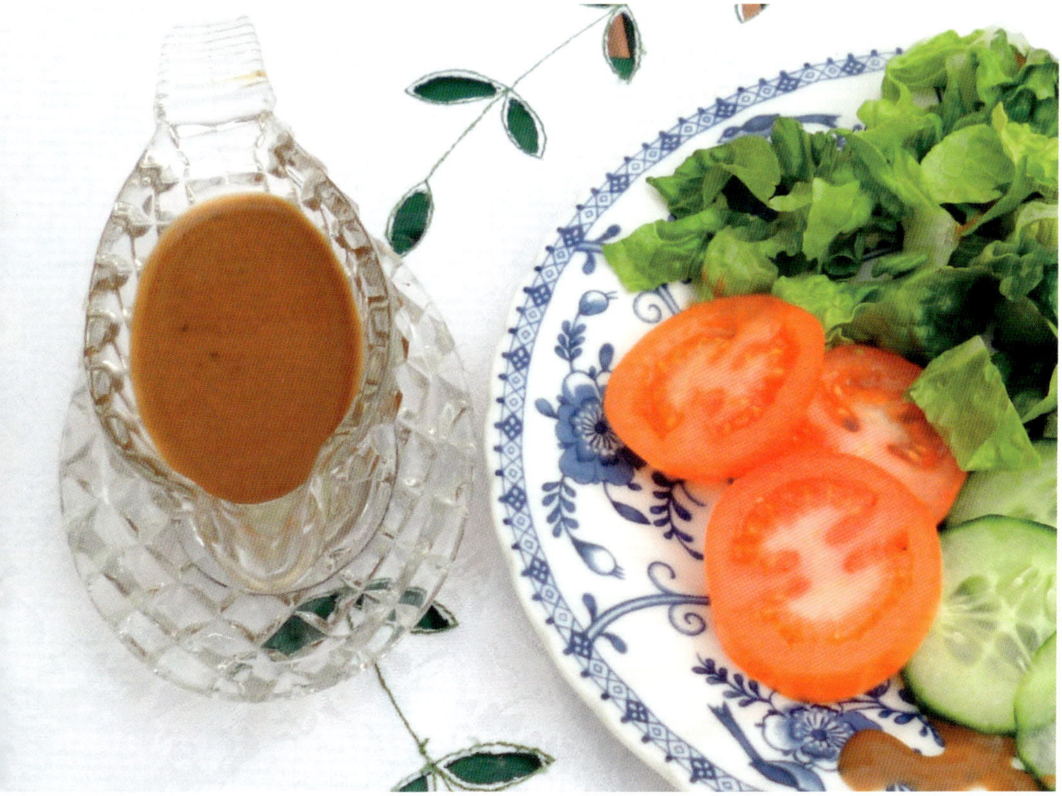

## Herb and Celery Light Dressing

**Ingredients:**

**Lemon peel and lemon juice of half a lemon**
**2 sprigs fresh tarragon (chopped finely)**
**2 sprigs fresh coriander (chopped finely)**
**Pinch of sea salt**
**3 spring onions chopped small and cook in water**
**1 stick celery (chopped very small)**
**Little black pepper**

**Method:**

Mix the ingredients together.

Liquidise if preferred and pour onto your salad just before eating or alternatively put into a bowl so that everyone can help themselves when ready to pour over their own salad.

## Herb Salad with Lemon Oil Dressing

**Ingredients:**

**225g baby salad leaves (e.g. little gems)**
**1 sprig of flat-leaf parsley**
**1 sprig of tarragon**
**1 sprig of chives**
**1 sprig of fennel herb**
**1 sprig of dill**
**Lemon olive oil or extra virgin olive oil with a little lemon juice**

**Method:**

Mix the baby salad leaves with the chopped herb sprigs and simply drizzle over a little lemon olive oil or extra virgin olive oil with a little lemon juice.

Add salt and toss together.

No need for vinegar or pepper with this dressing.

5

## Egg and Sweet Almond Oil Dressing

**Ingredients:**

1 tablespoon castor sugar
1 teaspoon English mustard
2 teaspoon olive oil or sweet almond oil
150ml malt vinegar
150ml milk
Pinch of salt
2 yolks of 2 hard-boiled eggs

**Method:**

Mix all together in a bowl until creamy and pour into a cooled sterilised bottle.

Keep in the fridge.

Shake well before using.

## Creamy Salad Dressing

**Ingredients:**

1 dessertspoon Dijon mustard
1 tablespoon plain flour
2 eggs
1 cupful milk
1 cupful vinegar
1 teaspoon salt
Pinch of pepper
2 tablespoon sugar
1 cupful water

**Method:**

Place all the ingredients into a saucepan and bring to the boil stirring all the time until thickened, as required.

Remove let cool and put into a sterilised bottle or jar.

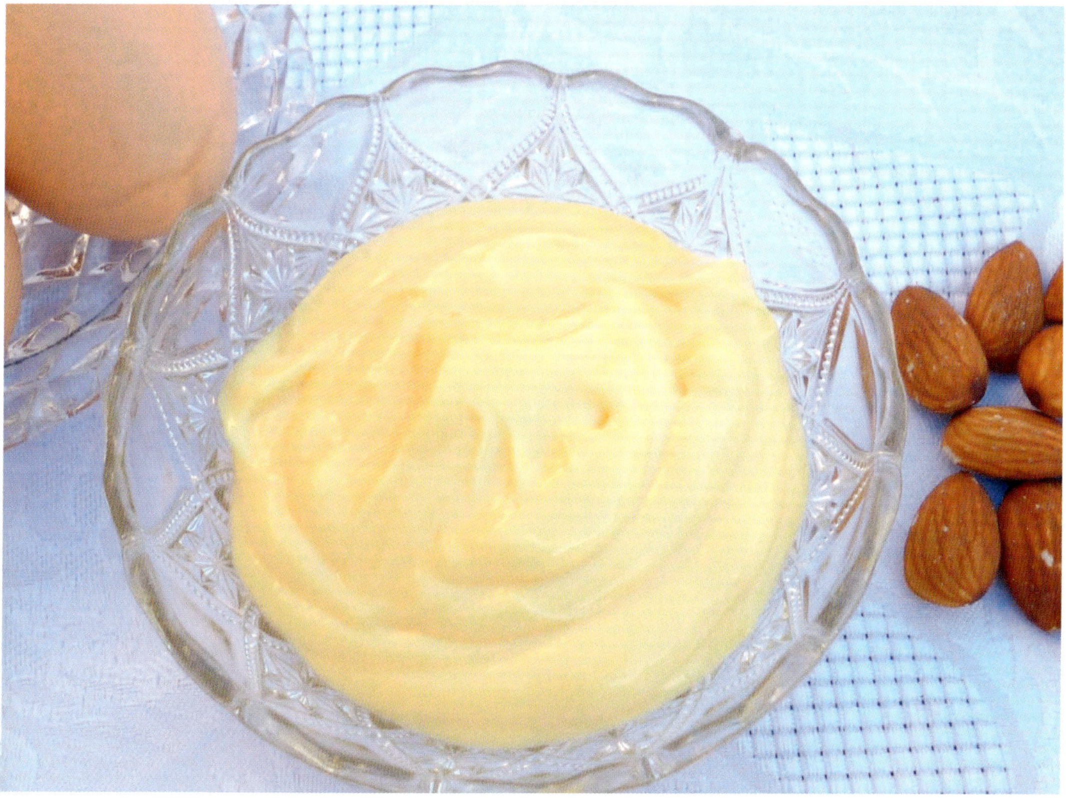

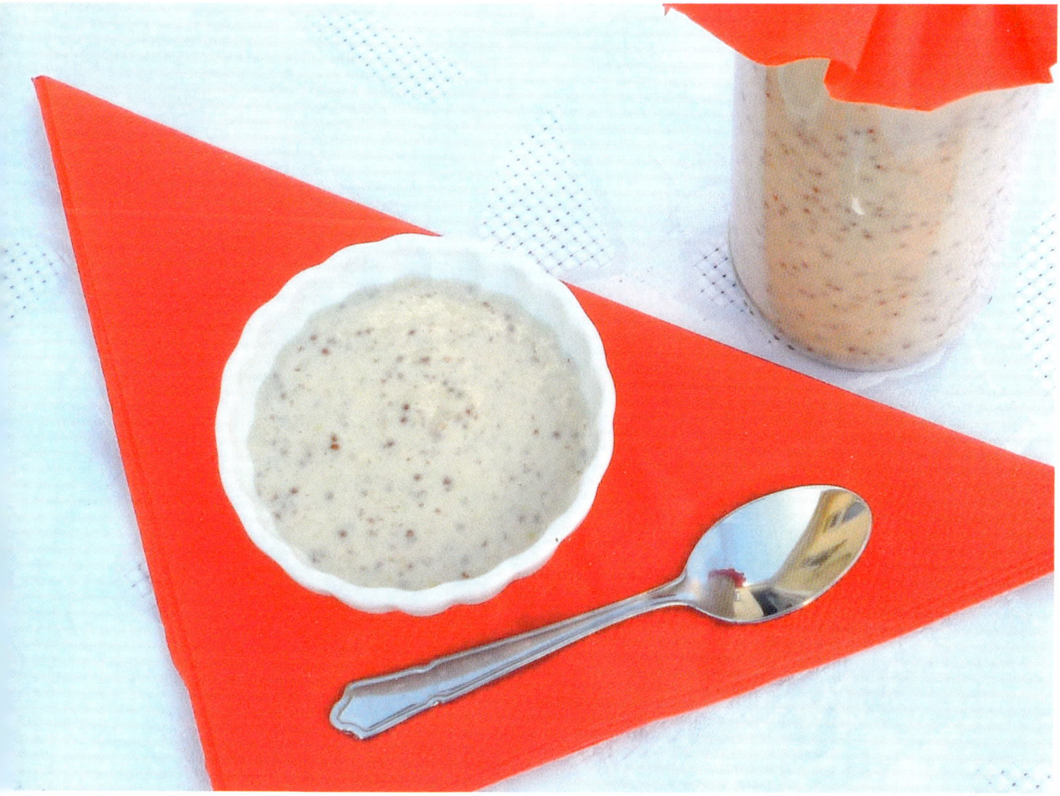

## Olive Oil Dressing
for soft green lettuce

**Ingredients:**

**1 tablespoon white wine vinegar**
**4 tablespoons olive oil**
**Quarter teaspoon caster sugar**
**Pinch of mashed garlic**
**Little salt**
**225g of soft lettuce (not ice-burg lettuce)**

**Method:**

Wash and dry lettuce.

Just before serving whisk the white wine vinegar, olive oil, caster sugar, mashed garlic and salt together and drizzle this over the leaves and toss gently ready to eat.

## Mother's Salad Cream

**Ingredients:**

50g margarine/butter
1 teaspoon English mustard
1 egg
1 egg yolk
1 cupful milk
1 teaspoon salt
Pinch of pepper
1 teaspoon plain flour
Half cupful vinegar

**Method:**

Put salt, pepper, flour, sugar and mustard in a bowl with a little milk and mix.

Put margarine/butter in a saucepan and melt, add well-beaten egg. Mix vinegar, then cupful of milk with other ingredients mix together.

Cook in saucepan and stir until it thickens. Remove from heat stirring all the time. When cold it is ready for use.

If sealed will keep for several weeks.

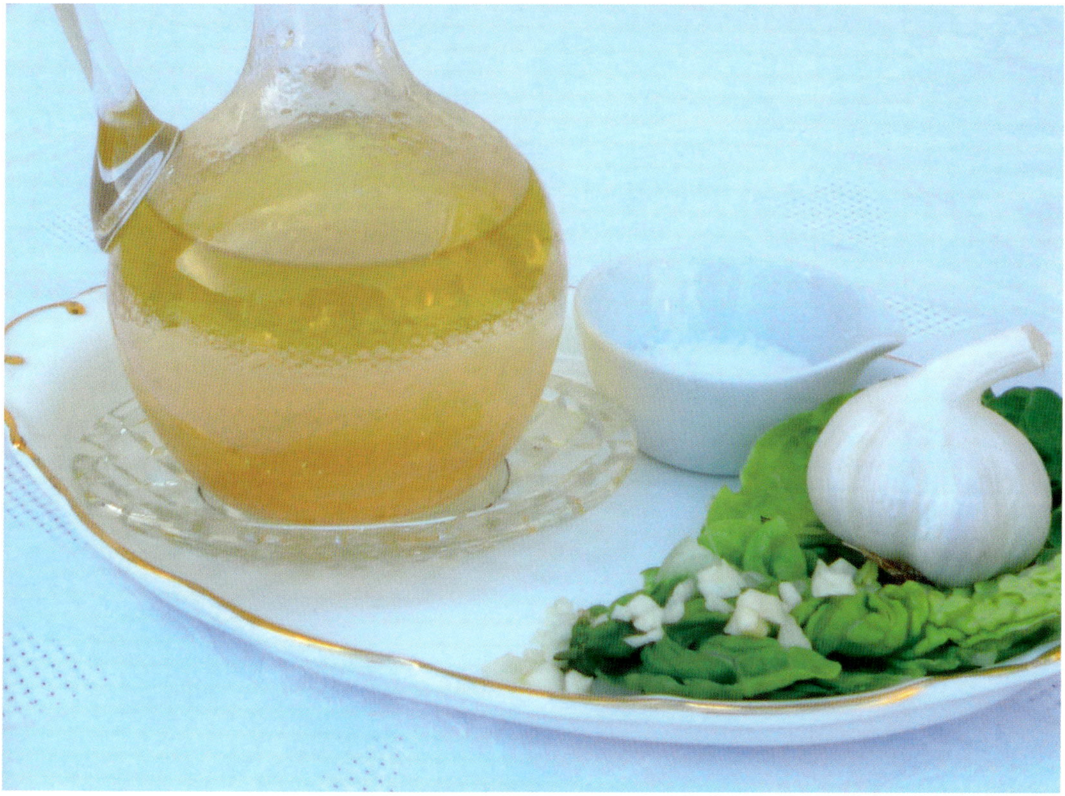

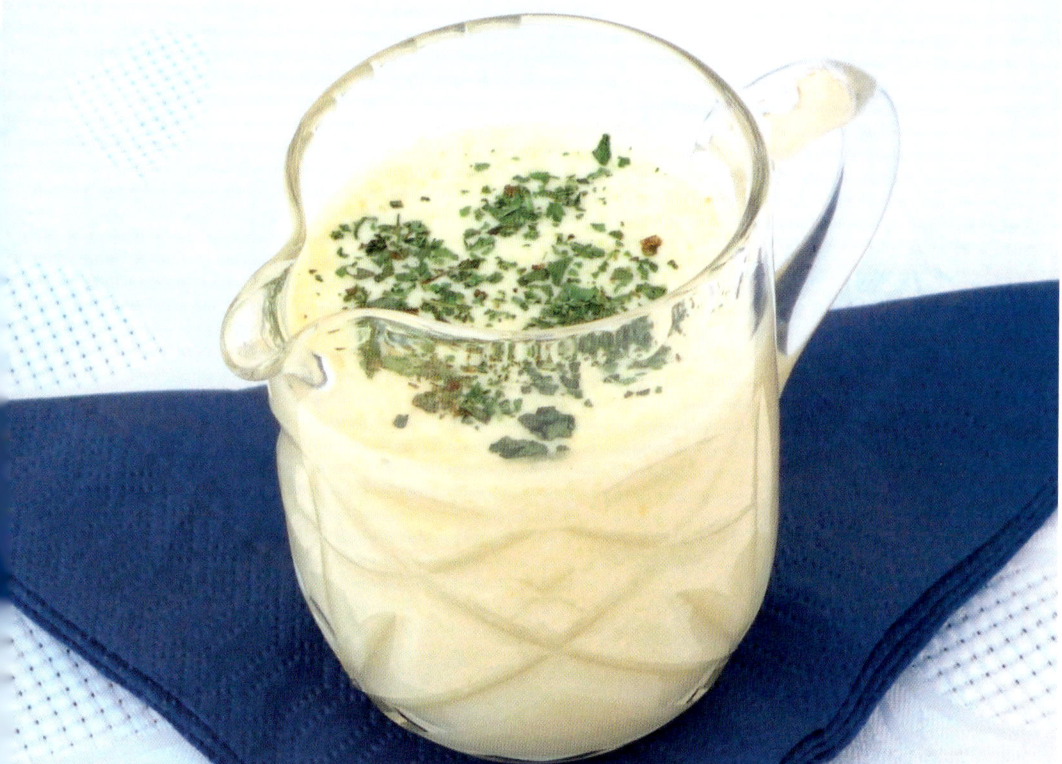

## Mustard Mayonnaise Sauce

**Ingredients:**

**2 egg yolks**
**1 teaspoon dry English mustard powder**
**1 teaspoon sugar**
**1 tablespoon white wine vinegar or lemon juice**
**6fl oz/175ml walnut oil or olive oil**
**Pinch of salt and pepper**

Method:

Make sure the ingredients are at room temperature then place the egg yolks, mustard powder, sugar, wine vinegar or lemon juice, salt and pepper into a bowl and liquidize together.

Use electric mixer, adding the oil slowly until the consistency is creamy.

## Garlic and Sherry Vinegar Dressing

**Ingredients:**

**6 tablespoons of extra virgin olive oil**
**1 clove of garlic**
**4 teaspoons sherry vinegar**
**Salt to taste**

Method:

Gently heat the extra virgin olive oil in a pan, add the finely chopped clove of garlic.

Cook for a few seconds until the garlic starts to colour.

Remove from heat and leave to cool, then whisk in the sherry vinegar and a little salt.

Just before serving spoon over a green salad. Sprinkle with freshly ground black pepper if desired.

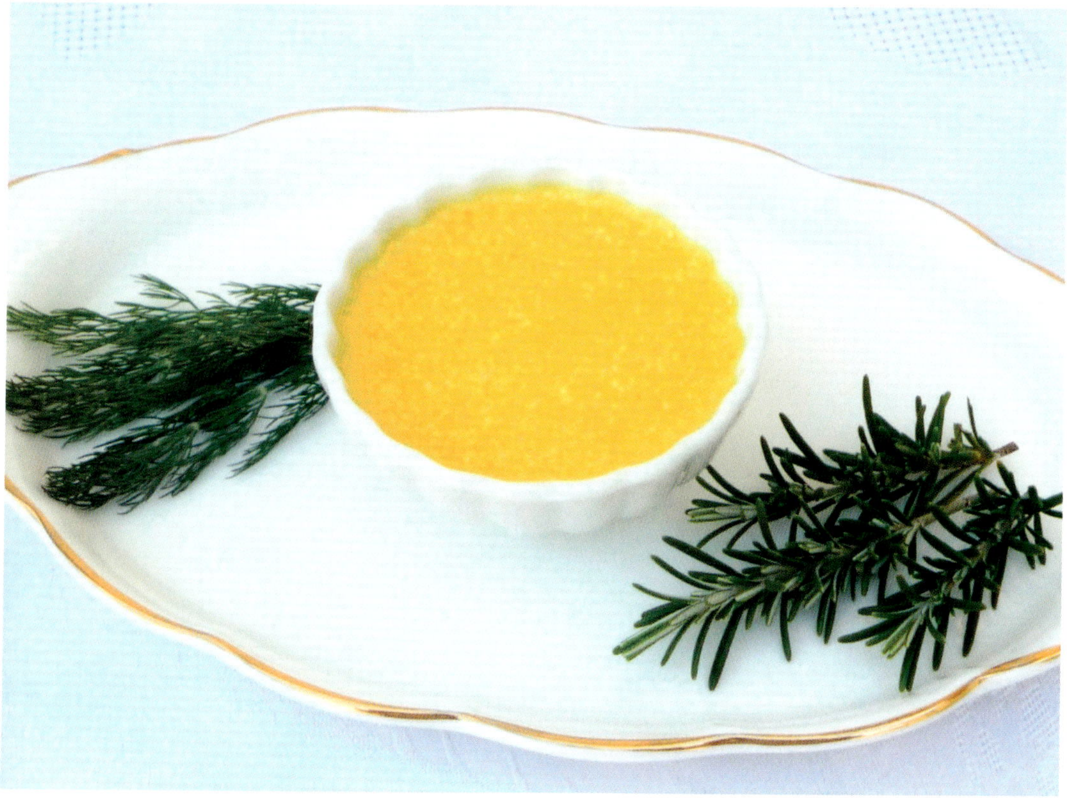

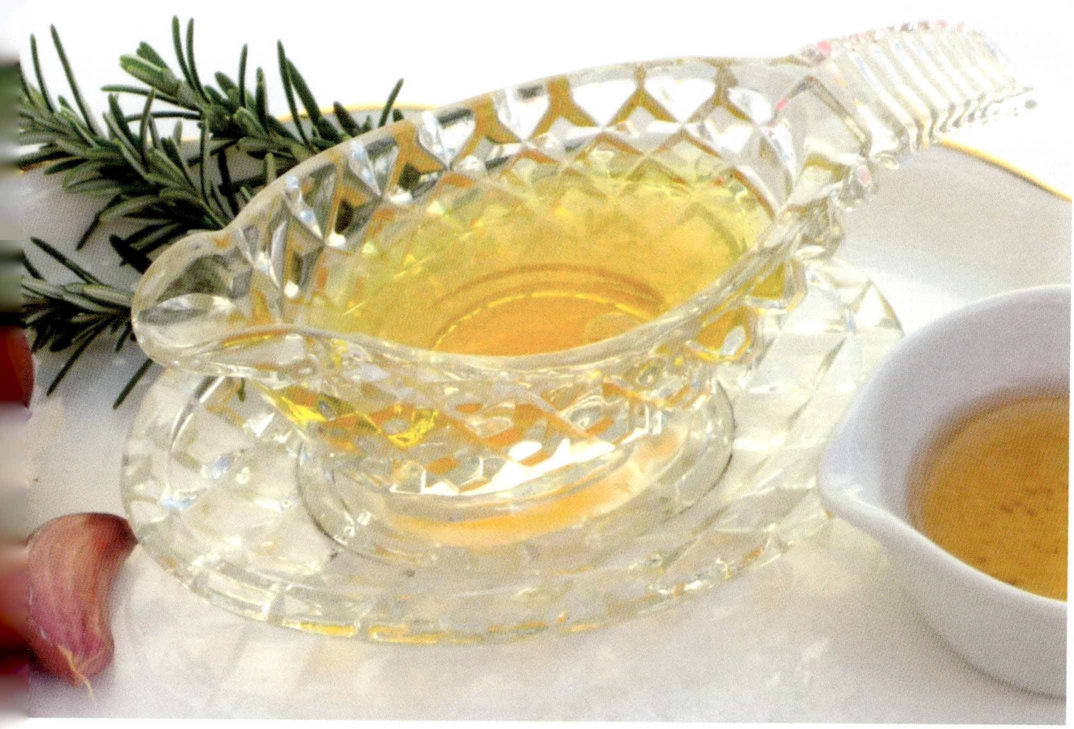

# Homemade Mayonnaise

Ingredients:

2 egg yolks
Half an onion, finely chopped
1 teaspoon English mustard
Three quarter teaspoon salt

Small pinch milled pepper
275ml/10fl oz olive oil
2 teaspoons white wine vinegar

Method:

Make sure all the ingredients are at room temperature.

Put the egg yolks, very finely chopped onion and English mustard into a bowl and whisk together.

Then carefully add the olive oil one drop at a time and whisk well until it thickens. You can put bigger drops of oil into the mixture, be careful not to let the ingredients separate at this stage.

When half the oil is in and the mixture has thickened add a little of the vinegar to thin the mixture a little, then add the rest of the oil whisking all the time, add the salt and pepper and if more vinegar is needed to thin the mixture then add a little more.

Note: Curdling happens if you add the oil too fast at the beginning so always begin drop by drop and then when it thickens you can add a little more.

This mayonnaise will keep in the fridge for about a week in a sealed container.

## Tomato, Basil and Red Onion Side Dressing

**Ingredients:**

**450g large beef tomatoes**
**3 tablespoons chopped red onion or shallot**
**12 finely shredded basil leaves**
**1 teaspoon white wine vinegar**
**5 teaspoons of extra virgin olive oil**
**Some salt and freshly ground black pepper**

**Method:**

Slice the tomatoes and arrange them in a shallow dish.

Sprinkle the chopped red onion or shallot and shredded basil leaves.

Then separately whisk together the white wine vinegar, extra virgin oil, salt and pepper.

Drizzle this over the tomatoes, onion/shallot and basil leaves just before serving.


## Thyme and Sour Cream Dressing
for beetroot, cucumber or any bean salad

**Ingredients:**

**4fl oz/150ml sour cream**
**1 tablespoon olive oil**
**2 tablespoons thyme**
**salt and pepper**
**1 teaspoon lemon juice**

**Method:**

Cut up the thyme finely and mix in a jar with the olive oil, lemon juice.

Shake well so that the oil breaks up and emulsifies with the lemon juice.

Stir into the sour cream and season with salt and pepper.

This makes a lovely dressing.

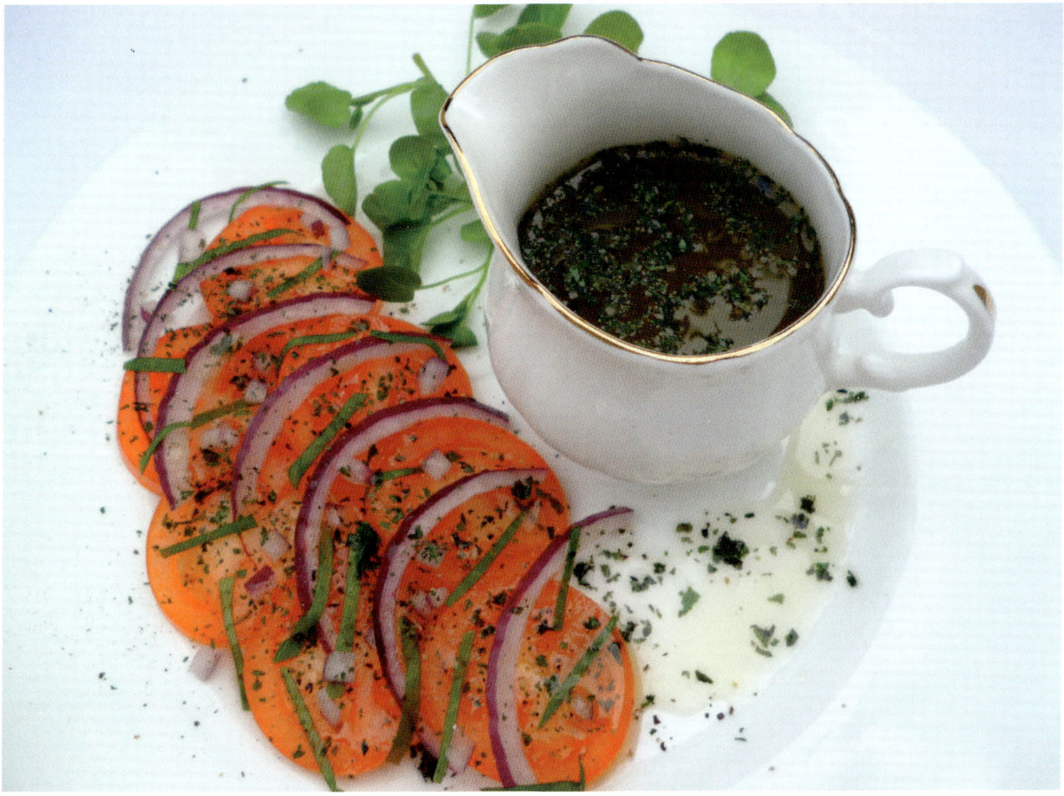

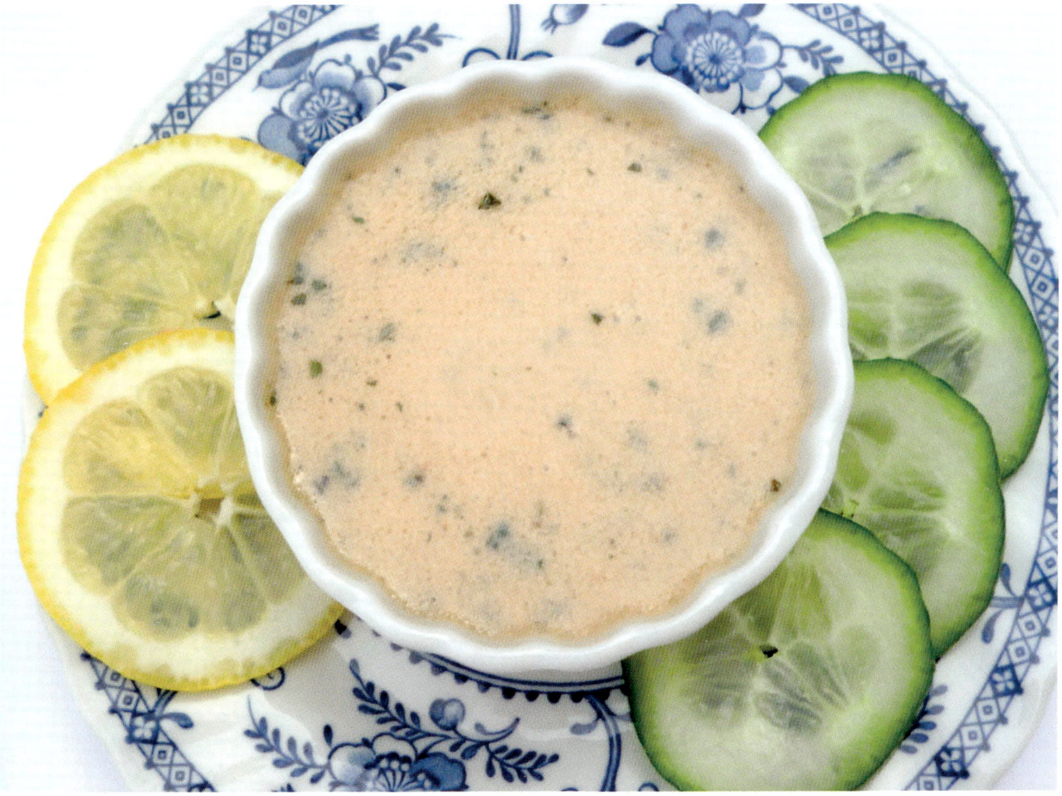

## Watercress Cream
goes well with mixed vegetable fritters

**Ingredients:**

**85g watercress, trimmed and chopped**
**Juice of half a lemon**
**200g Greek-style yoghurt**

Method:

Stir the chopped watercress and lemon juice into the yoghurt.

Spoon into a serving bowl, cover and keep chilled.

A very refreshing, healthy dip.

## Balsamic and Garlic Dressing
for grilled peppers, tomatoes and olive salad

**Ingredients:**

**90ml/6 tablespoons extra-virgin olive oil**
**2 cloves garlic, finely chopped**
**30ml/2 tablespoons balsamic or wine vinegar**
**Salt and ground black pepper**

Method:

Mix the oil and garlic together in a small bowl, crushing the garlic with a spoon to release the flavour.

Mix in the vinegar and season with salt and pepper.

Pour over the dressing, mix well and allow to stand for at least 30 minutes before serving.

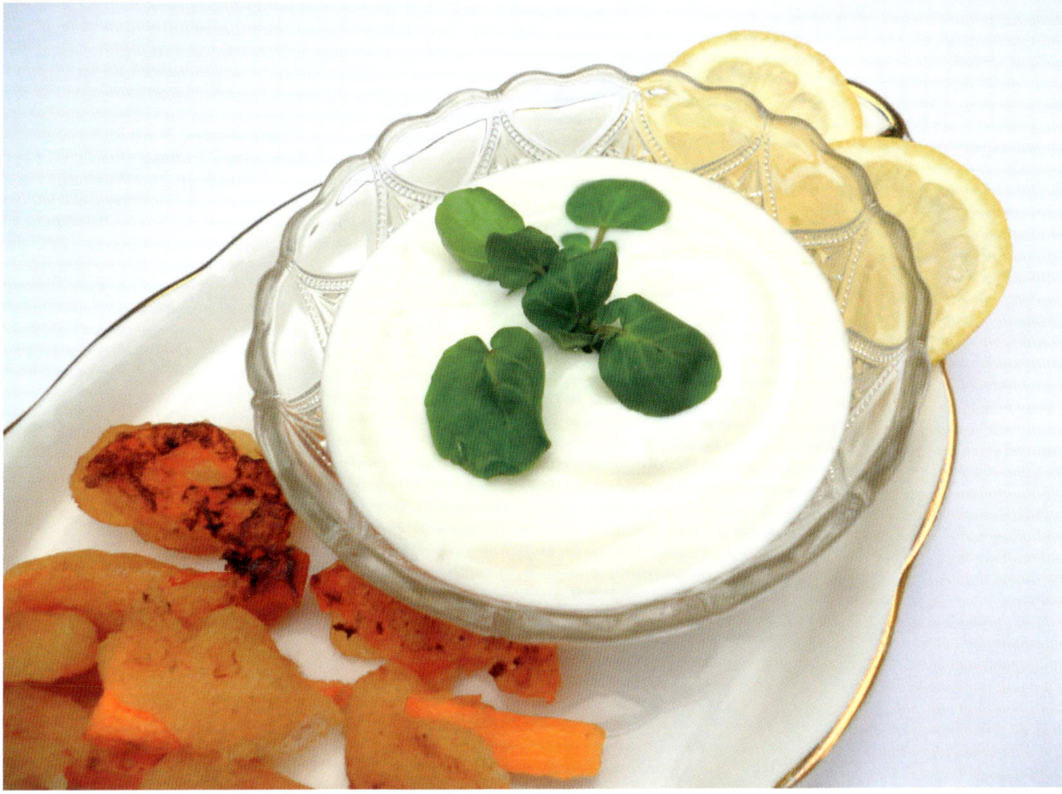

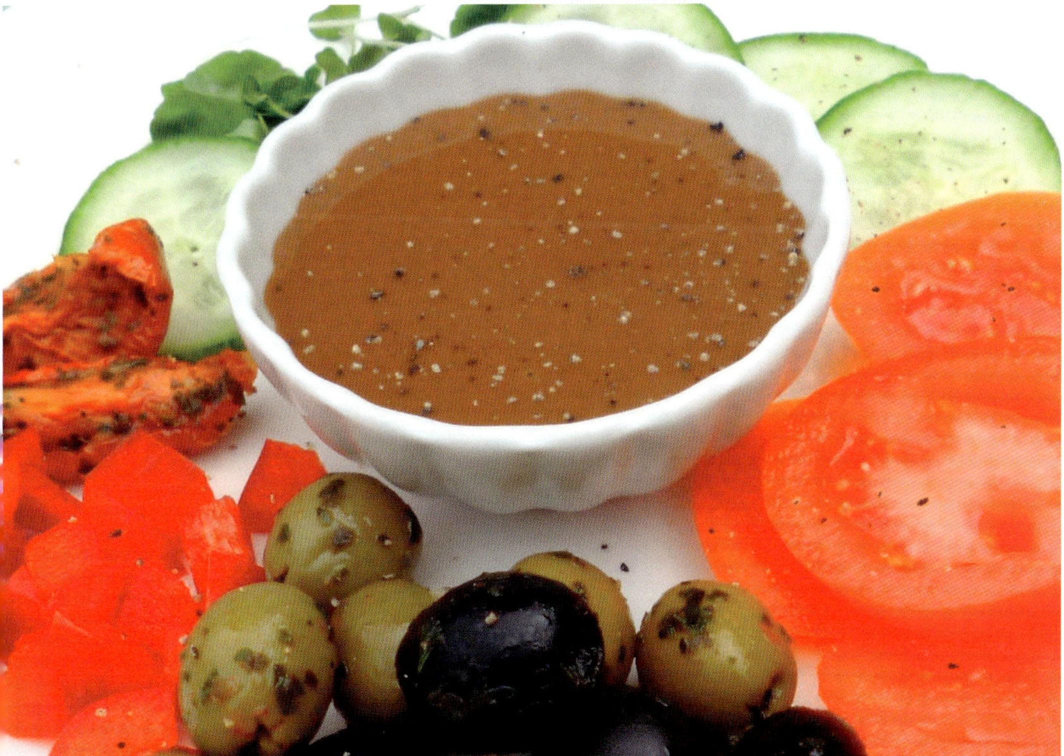

## Cashew and Apple Coleslaw Dressing

**Ingredients:**

**250g/8oz white cabbage**
**3 celery sticks**
**3 Red Delicious dessert apples**
**4 spring onions**
**50g/2oz cashew nuts, toasted**
**2 tablespoons chopped parsley**
**150ml mayonnaise**
**2 tablespoons natural yoghurt**

**Method:**

Shred the white cabbage, slice the celery sticks and spring onions. Core and thinly slice the dessert apples.

Put the shredded cabbage, sliced celery sticks, sliced apples, sliced spring onions, cashew nuts and parsley into a mixing bowl.

Mix the mayonnaise and yoghurt together then add to the mixing bowl and toss thoroughly.

Transfer to a clean bowl ready to serve.

## Tomato and Yoghurt Dressing

**Ingredients:**

**300g/10ozs natural yoghurt**
**2 tablespoons chopped basil**
**500g/1lb tomatoes, skinned and cut very small.**

**Method:**

Put the yoghurt together with the chopped basil into a bowl, add salt and pepper to taste and mix well.

Stir in the pieces of tomato, then transfer to a serving dish.

Keep in the fridge for 30 minutes before serving.

This make a delicious refreshing, accompaniment to green salad in summer.

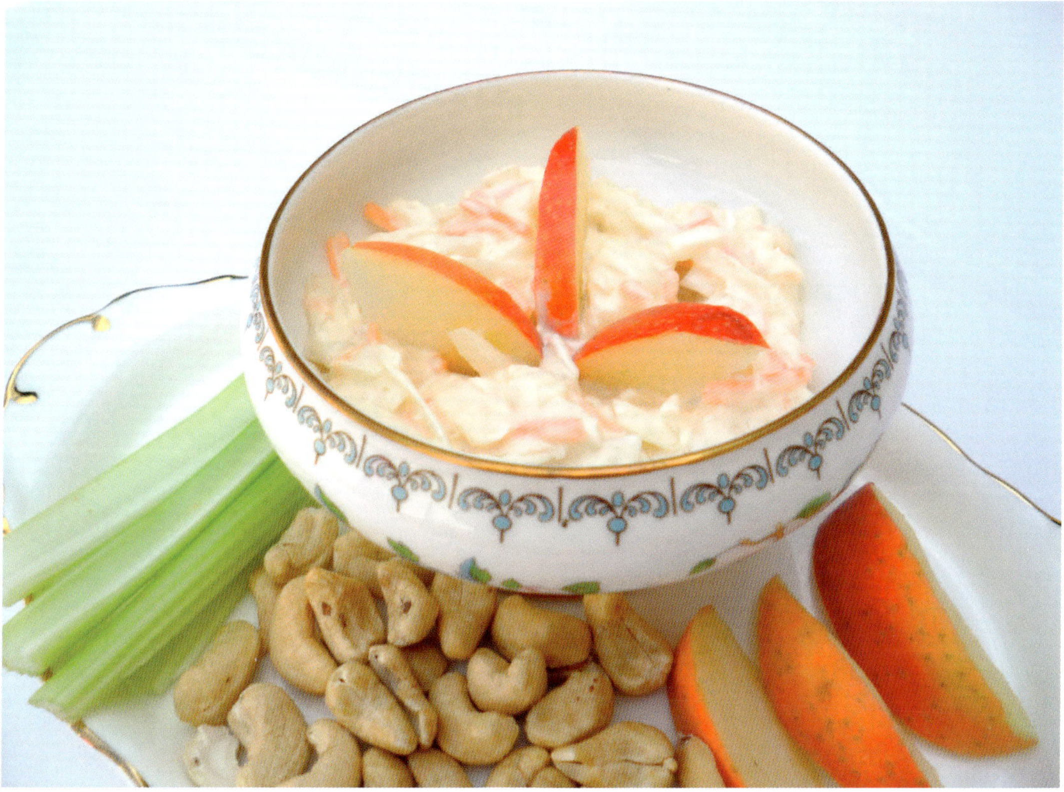

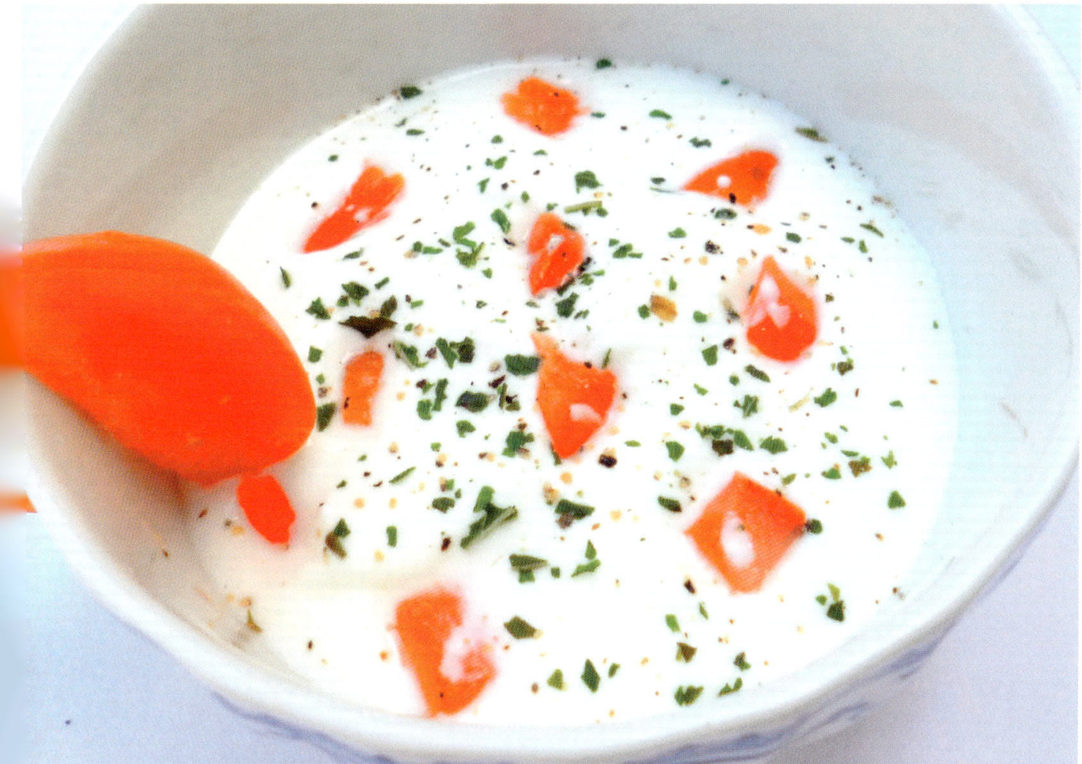

# Rich Cheese and Onion Sauce

**Ingredients:**

**115g/4oz cottage cheese**
**50g/2oz blue cheese**
**1 tablespoon single cream**
**1 onion, finely chopped**

**1 teaspoon chopped chives**
**1 green pepper, fine chopped and de-seeded**
**1 finely chopped stick of celery**
**Small pinch of salt.**

Method:

Crumble the blue cheese into a bowl add the cottage cheese, cream, onion and salt. Beat to a smooth consistency.

Stir in the chopped chives, green pepper and celery. If preferred just blended with a blender to create a finer texture.

Cover and put in a cool place overnight to let the flavour develop.

# ~ Fish ~

## Freshwater Fish Marinade

**Ingredients:**

**3 black and 3 green olives cut in four (remove stones if necessary)**
**Capers cut in half**
**Half a teaspoon fish seasoning**
**A little pepper**
**2 tablespoons olive oil**

**Method:**

Put the cut olives and capers into a bowl, mix in the olive oil, fish seasoning, pepper and place over the fish.

Sprinkle with oregano and tarragon and place in the oven to bake for 20 minutes at Gas mark 4 / 180°C / 350°F.

## Tarragon and Celery Sauce
add to fish when eating

**Ingredients:**

**Half a lemon**
**1 sprig fresh tarragon finely chopped**
**1 sprig fresh parsley finely chopped**
**Pinch of salt**
**1 onion**
**2 tablespoons cold milk.**
**1 teaspoon of cornflour**
**1 stick celery**

**Method:**

Juice and zest the lemon half. Remove stringy skin from celery and finely chop.

Chop the onion and cook in water until tender. Then allow to cool. Drain water into separate container.

Place all the ingredients into a bowl, except the onion water and chop by hand or liquidize.

Add 2 tablespoons of the cooled water from the onion and the milk and the corn flour, mix well and heat for mins stirring all the time until the mixture thickens.

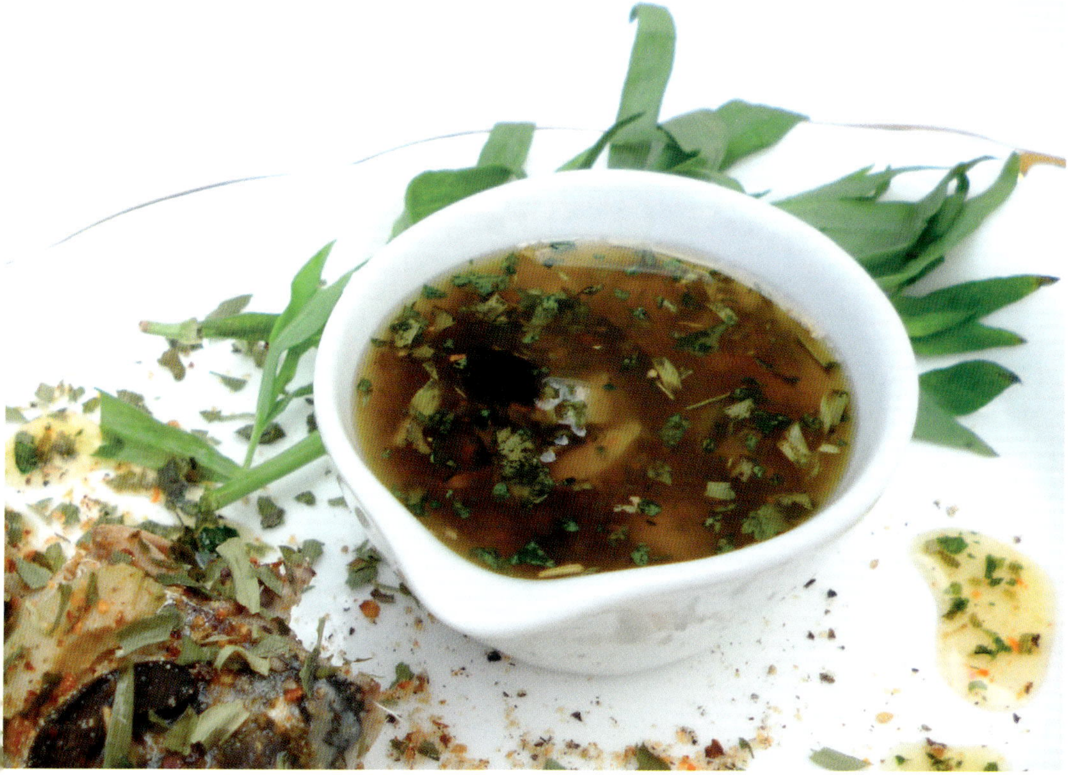

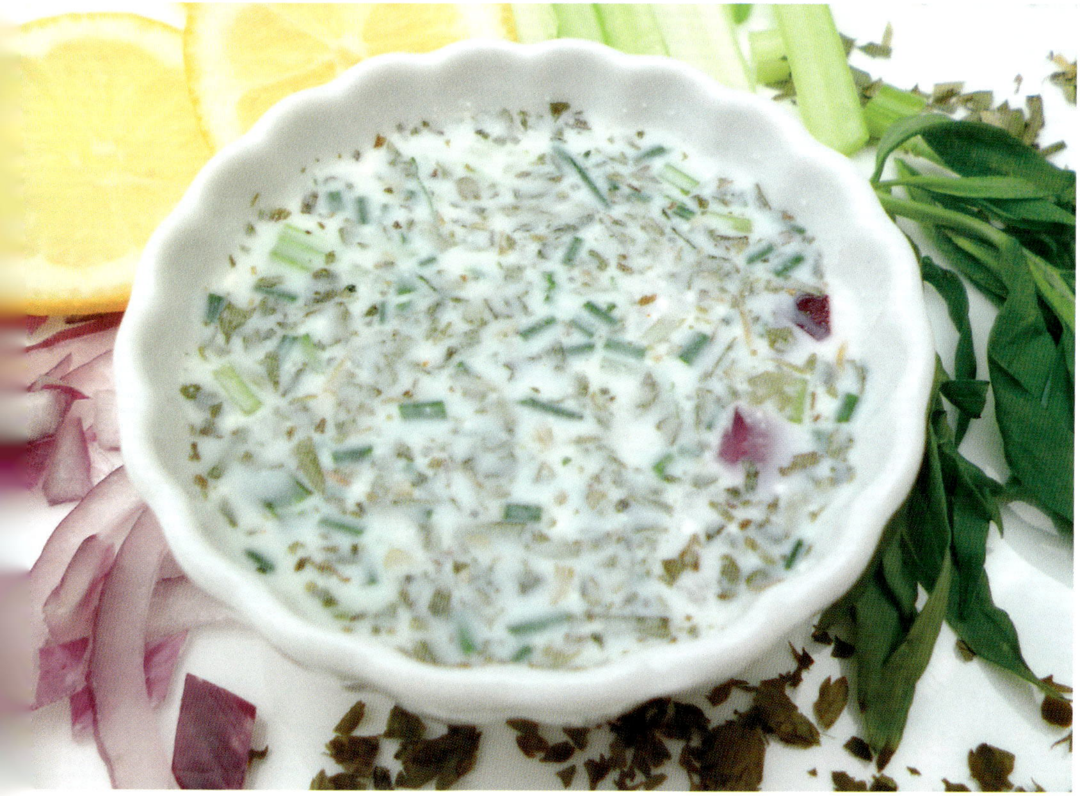

## Creamy White Sauce
for fish or seafood

**Ingredients:**

**600ml/two and a half cups of white wine**
**1 teaspoon paprika**
**2 teaspoons lemon juice**
**2 cloves garlic, crushed**
**12fl oz/375ml fromage frais**
**1 tablespoon chopped fresh dill**
**Pinch of pepper**

**Method:**

Wine, paprika, lemon juice and garlic in a saucepan and bring to the boil, strain liquid through a sieve and stir fromage frais into the mixture and bring to the boil.

Reduce heat and simmer for 10 minutes.

Add dill and black pepper.

Serve on cooked fish or seafood.


## Lime and Turmeric Mayonnaise for Fish

**Ingredients:**

**2 tablespoon hot fish stock or chicken stock**
**1 teaspoon tarragon**
**185ml/6 fl oz mayonnaise**
**A quarter teaspoon saffron threads**
**A quarter teaspoon ground turmeric**
**1 tablespoon lime juice**
**Pinch of pepper**

**Method:**

Place stock and saffron threads in a bowl and set aside to steep for 10 minutes. Strain stock mixture.

Place stock mixture, mayonnaise, turmeric, lime juice and black pepper to taste in a bowl and mix to combine.

Cover and chill until ready to serve.

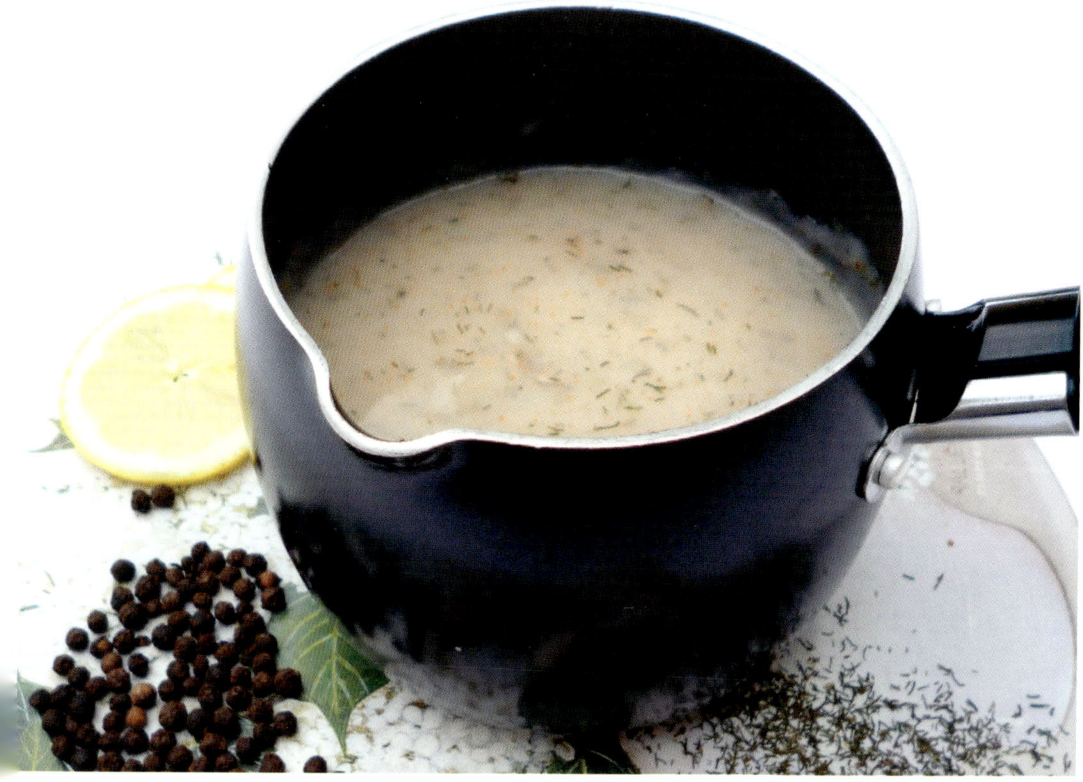

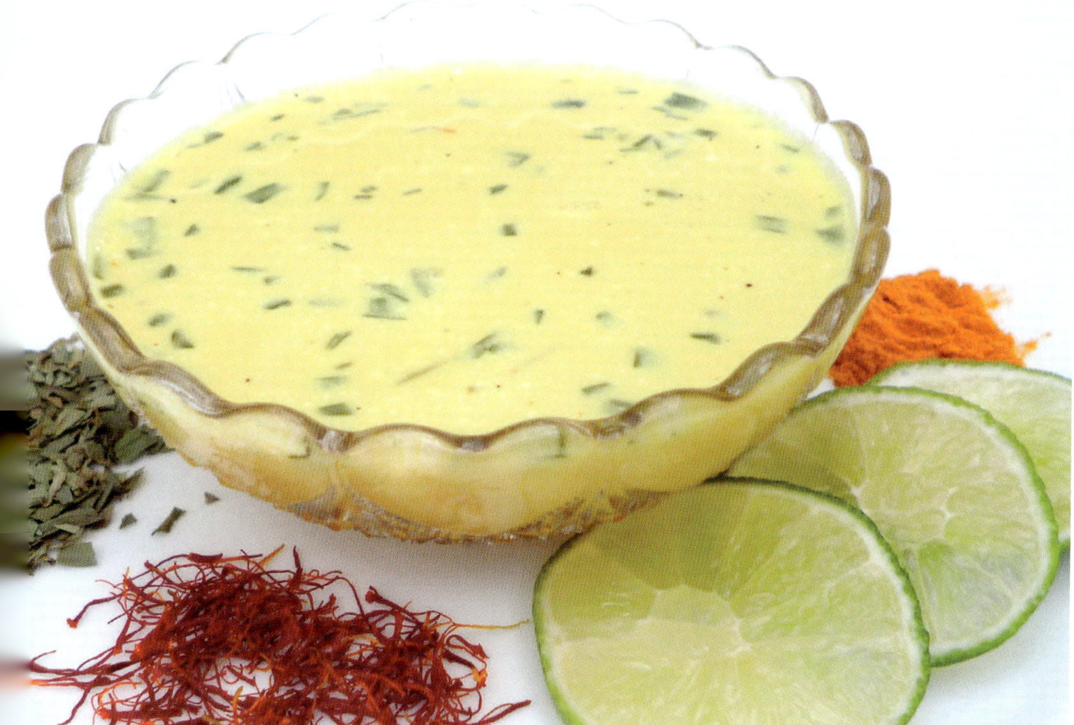

# Hollandaise Sauce

**Ingredients:**

2 egg yolks
1 onion chopped
225g of unsalted butter
Juice of half a lemon

A little pinch of cayenne pepper
Half a teaspoon salt
2 tablespoon water

Method:

Firstly, place the butter in a small pan and leave it over a very low heat until it has melted.

Then skim off any scum from the surface and pour off the clear clarified butter into a bowl, leaving behind the milky white solids that will have settled on the bottom of the pan.

Place the water and egg yolks into a heat-proof bowl set over a plan of simmering water, check that the base of the bowl is not touching the water.

Whisk until creamy.

Remove the bowl from the pan and gradually whisk in the clarified butter until thick

Whisk in the lemon juice, cayenne pepper and salt.

This sauce is best used as soon as it is made but will hold for up to 2 hours if kept covered in a warm place, such as over a saucepan of warm water.

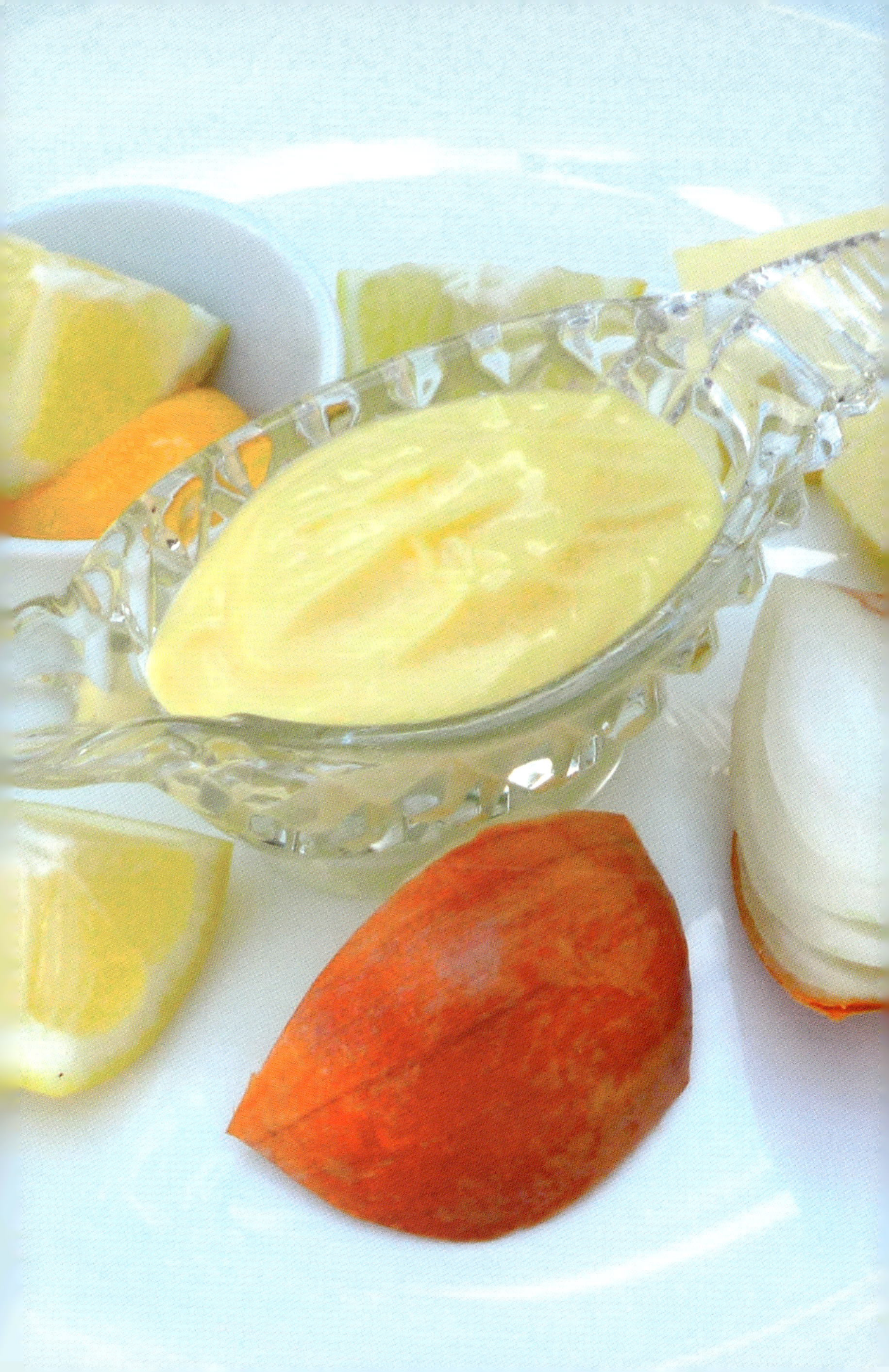

## Walnut and Herb Marinade
for mackerel

**Ingredients:**

6 leaves of fresh dill
2 sprigs of fresh parsley
1 tablespoon chopped chives
2 sprigs of rosemary
1 clove garlic
25g chopped walnuts
2 tablespoon olive oil
Pinch salt and pepper
1 teaspoon lemon juice
30g fresh bread crumbs

**Method:**

Oven preheat to 220°C, 425°F or gas mark 7.

Prepare the fish in your usual way.

Chop the herbs and garlic and mix with the chopped walnuts and add the oil.

Add the salt, pepper and lemon juice mix together and pour over the fish before cooking and sprinkle the breadcrumbs on top and bake in the oven for 15 minutes.

## General Tartar Sauce

**Ingredients:**

10fl oz/275ml mayonnaise
1 tablespoon of chopped capers
3 chopped gherkins
Sprig of chopped parsley
2 tablespoon single cream

**Method:**

Place the ingredients into a bowl.

Use an electric mixer to chop and blend for a few seconds.

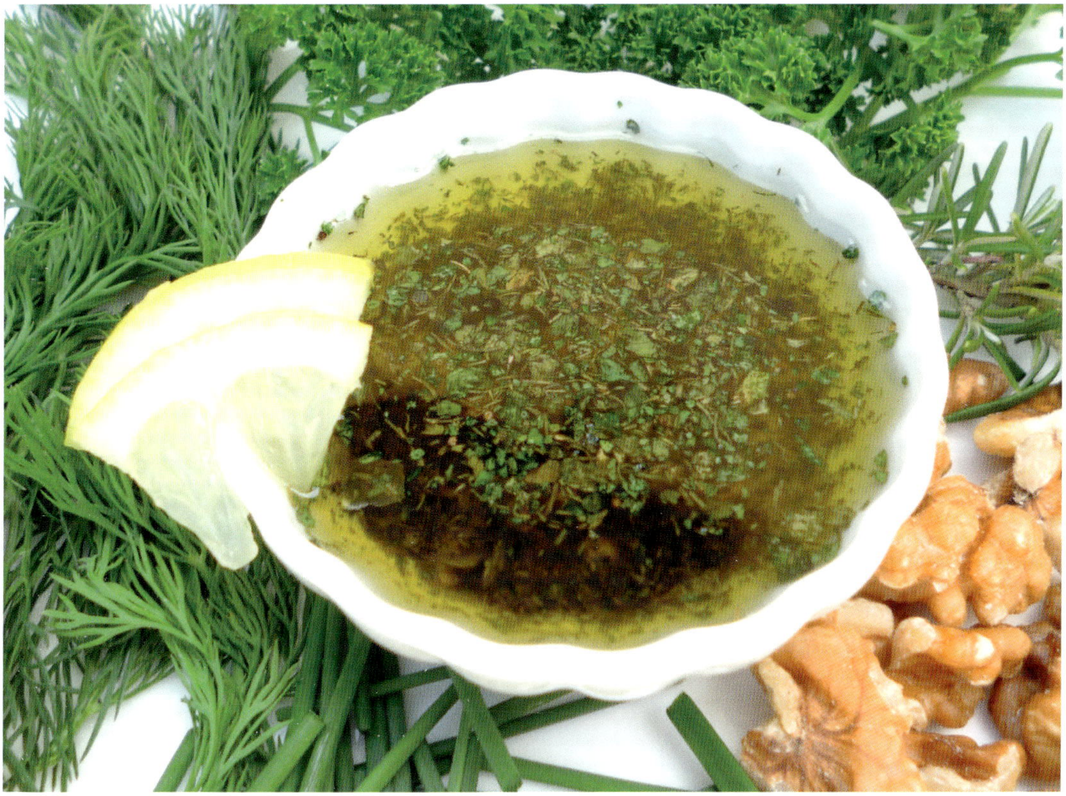

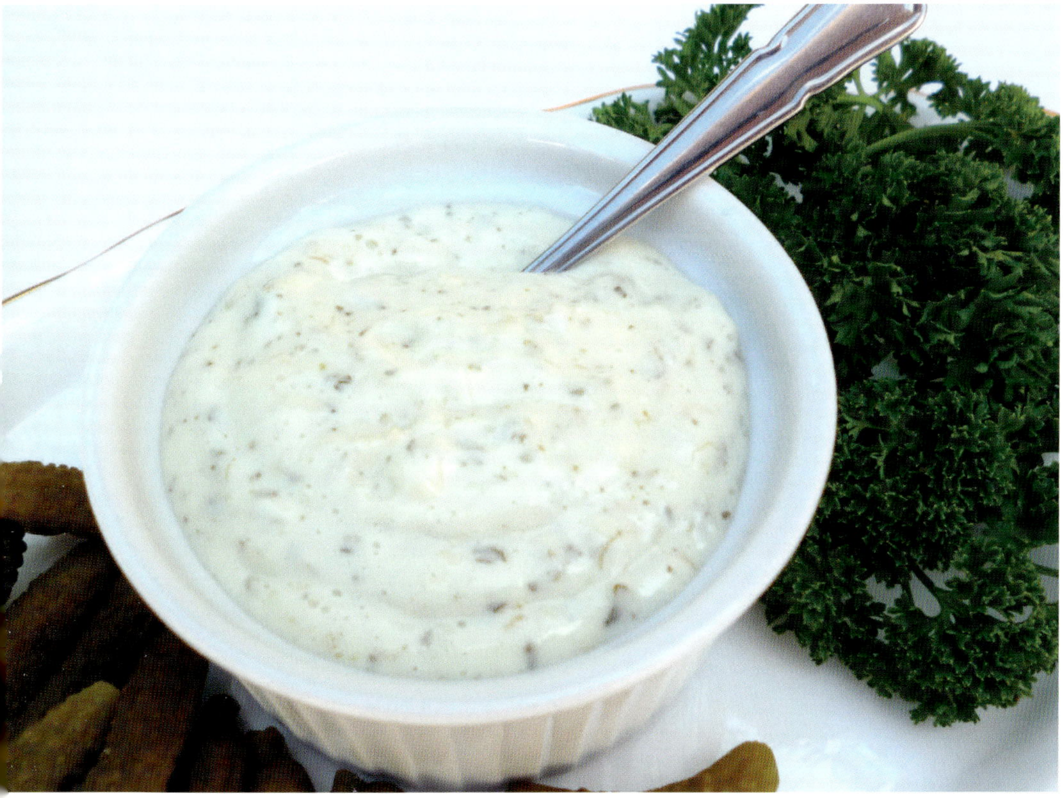

# Homemade White Sauce

**Ingredients:**

**15fl oz/450ml milk**
**40g butter or margarine**
**40g plain flour**
**Little salt and pepper to taste**

**Method:**

Place butter in a saucepan and melt, stir in the flour, making a roux. Stir well for about 3 minutes.

Remove from heat and put into a blender or mixer.

Heat the milk to simmering point.

Pour the milk onto the roux and blend for 30 seconds.

Pour back into the saucepan, stirring for 2 minutes add a little salt and pepper. Remove from heat ready for serving.

# Tomato and Coriander Sauce
for plaice

**Ingredients:**

**2 chopped spring onions**
**2 tablespoons chopped coriander**
**2 tomatoes chopped**
**Pinch of caster sugar**
**1 tablespoon white wine vinegar**
**Pinch of cayenne pepper**
**Pinch of salt**

**Method:**

Mix all the ingredients together and blitz to make sauce and put in a cool place until ready to serve over plaice fillets or similar fish.

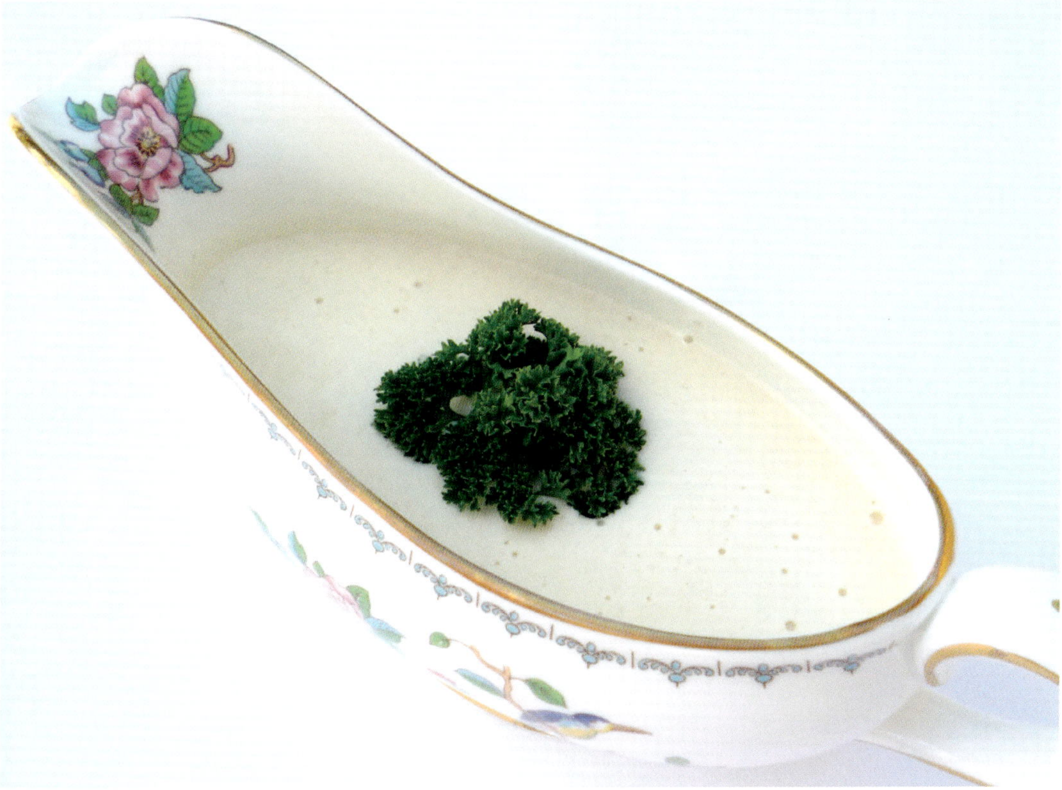

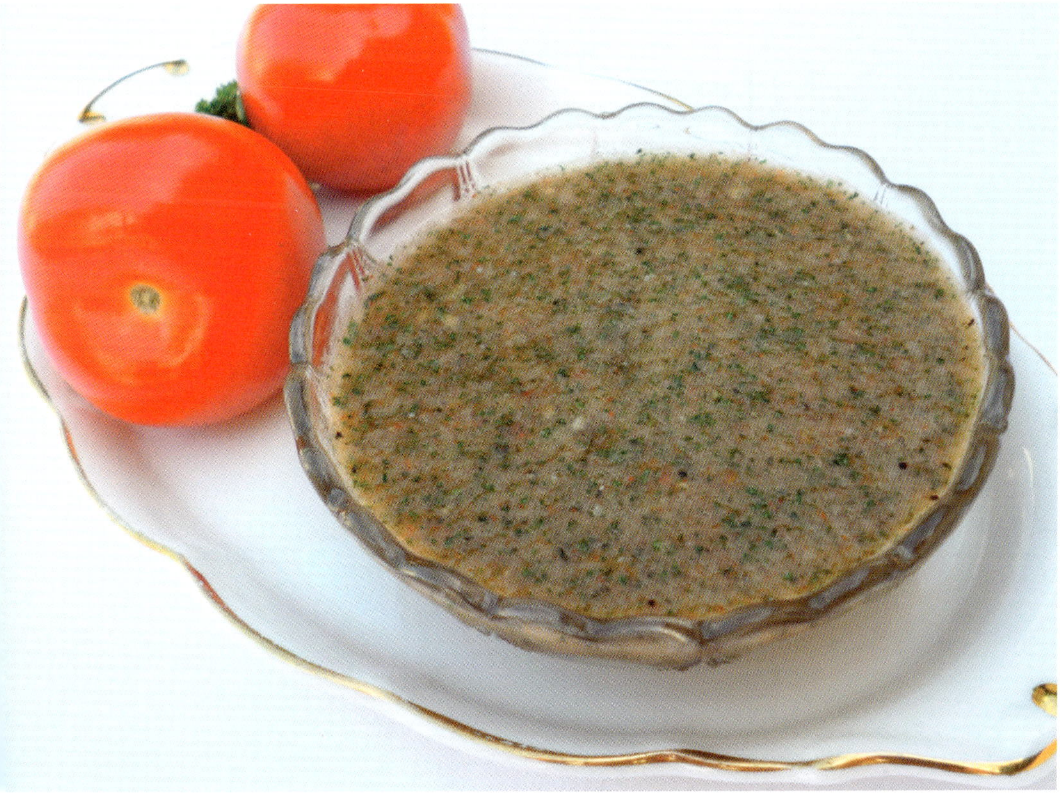

## Mustard and Garlic Dressing
for seafood salad

**Ingredients:**

**Method:**

**1 teaspoon white wine vinegar**
**1 teaspoon Dijon mustard**
**1 clove garlic, crushed**
**2 tablespoons olive oil**
**1 tablespoon natural yoghurt**
**Salt and pepper to taste**
**Slices of lemon to garnish**

Whisk the vinegar, mustard and crushed garlic then gradually whisk in the oil, add the natural yoghurt to make a slightly creamy dressing.

Add salt and pepper to taste and then gently stir it into the salad and garnish with slices of lemon.

## Homemade Parsley Sauce

**Ingredients:**

**Method:**

**2 - 3 sprigs freshly chopped parsley**
**Juice of half a lemon**
**15fl oz/425ml milk**
**40g butter or margarine**
**1 teaspoon plain flour**
**1 tablespoon single cream**
**Pinch salt and pepper**

Place the milk, cream, butter/margarine and flour into a saucepan and whisk while heating until thickens.

Then cook for 5 minutes stirring in the chopped parsley, lemon juice, salt and pepper.

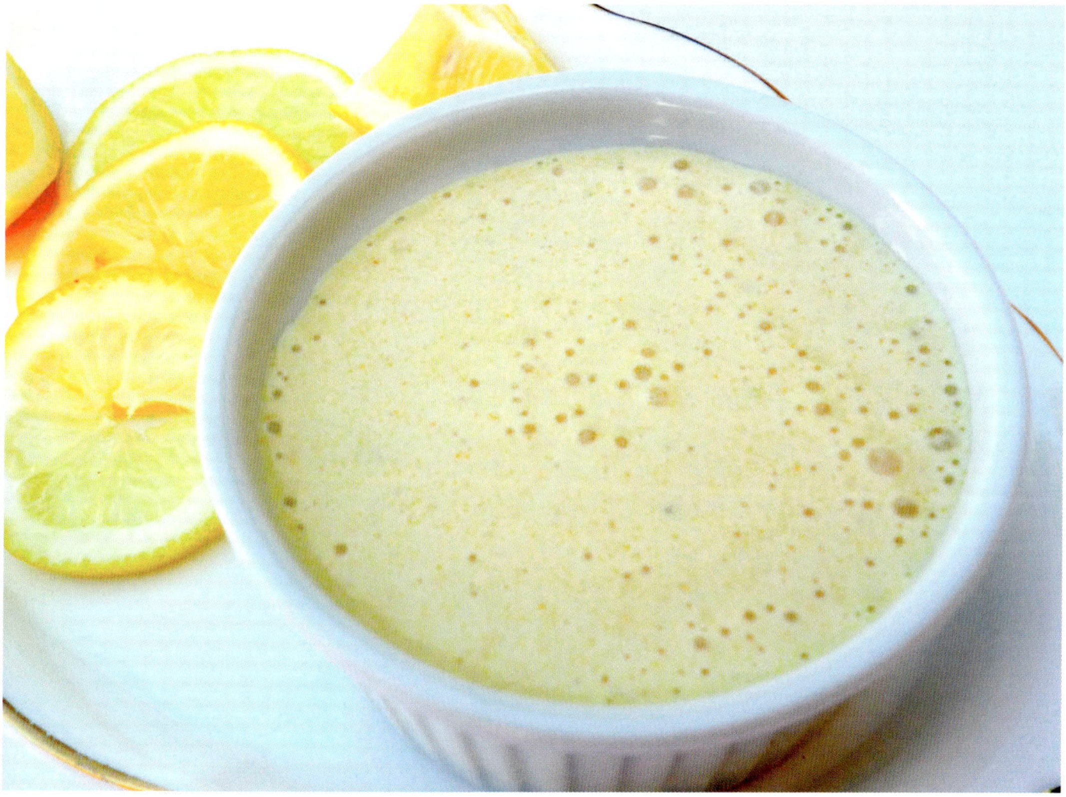

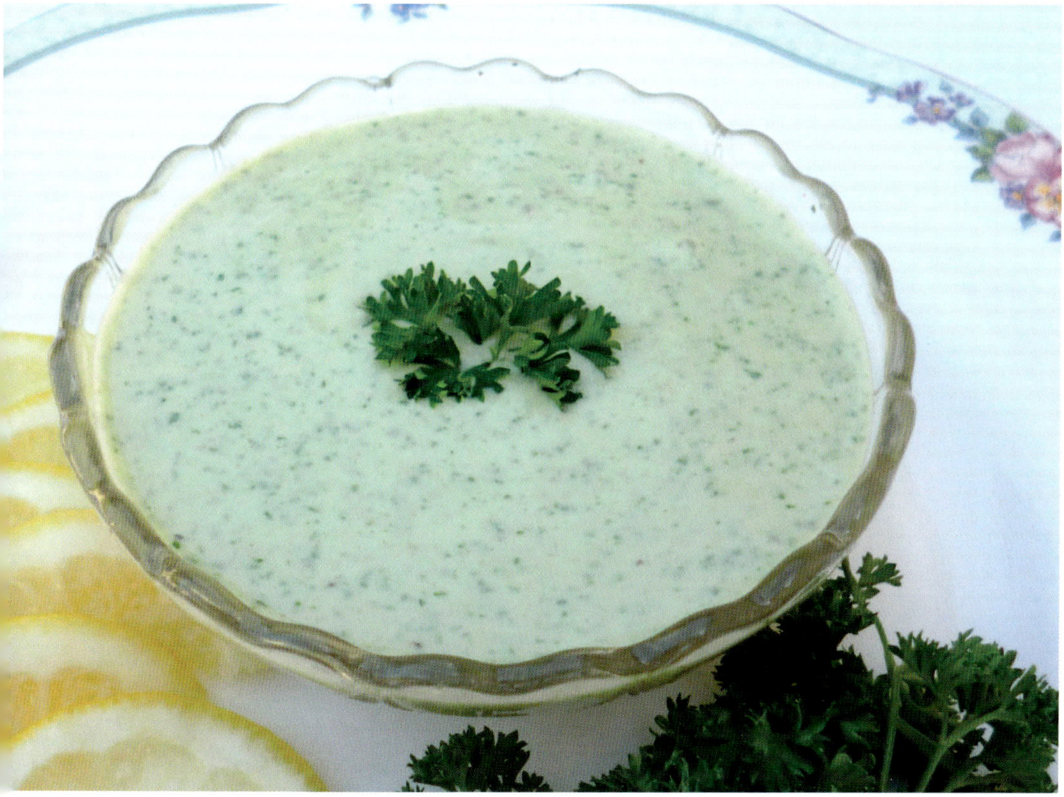

## Homemade Mornay Sauce

**Ingredients:**

**1 teaspoon of dry mustard**
**25g plain flour**
**10fl oz/275ml milk**
**10fl oz/275ml single cream**
**40g butter or margarine**
**75g grated cheddar cheese**
**Pinch of cayenne pepper**
**Juice of half a lemon**
**Little salt and pepper**

Method:

Place the milk, cream, mustard, flour and butter into a saucepan and heat, stirring until thickened.

Add the grated cheese and cook slowly for 5 minutes, stirring all the time.

Season with salt, pepper, cayenne and lemon juice.

Pour over baked fish.

## Mustard and Lemon Sauce
served with herrings

**Ingredients:**

**1 onion**
**40g butter or margarine**
**10fl oz/275ml milk**
**25g plain flour**
**2 teaspoon dry mustard**
**150ml stock**
**Juice of half a lemon**
**Little salt and pepper**

Method:

Chop the onion and add to the milk and bring to the boil and remove from heat.

Strain this liquid and add the butter, flour, mustard and stock and bring to the boil, stirring all the time.

Add the salt and pepper and cook for a five minutes and finally stirring in the lemon juice.

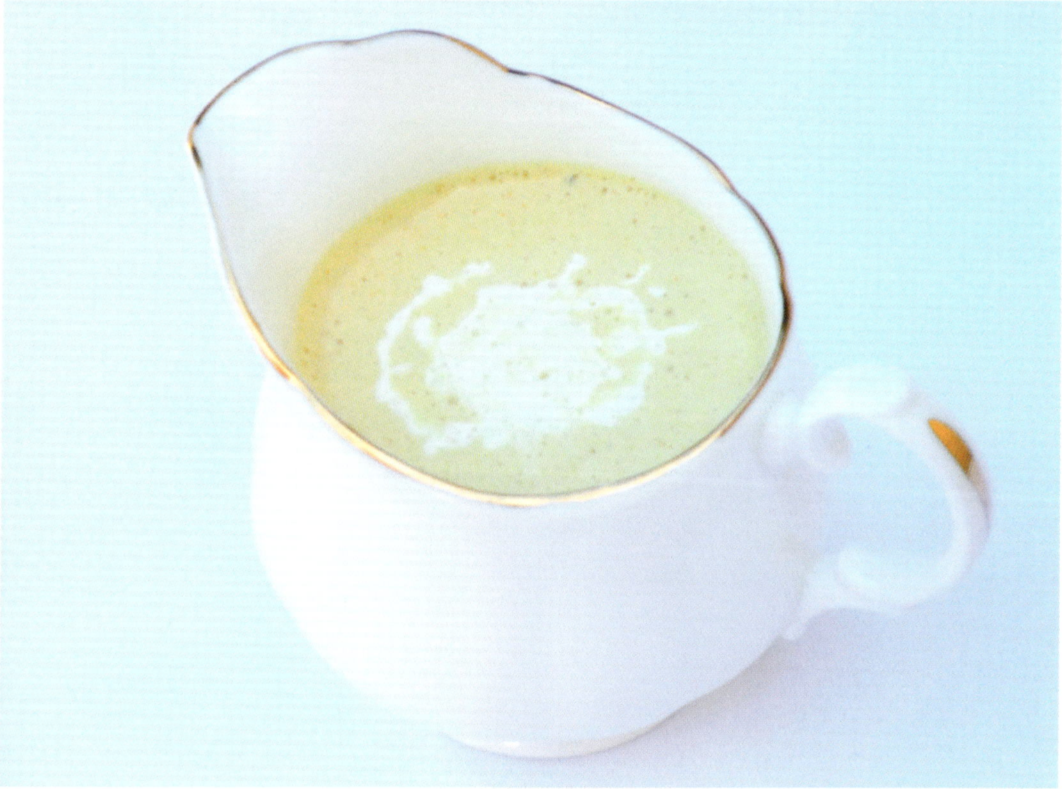

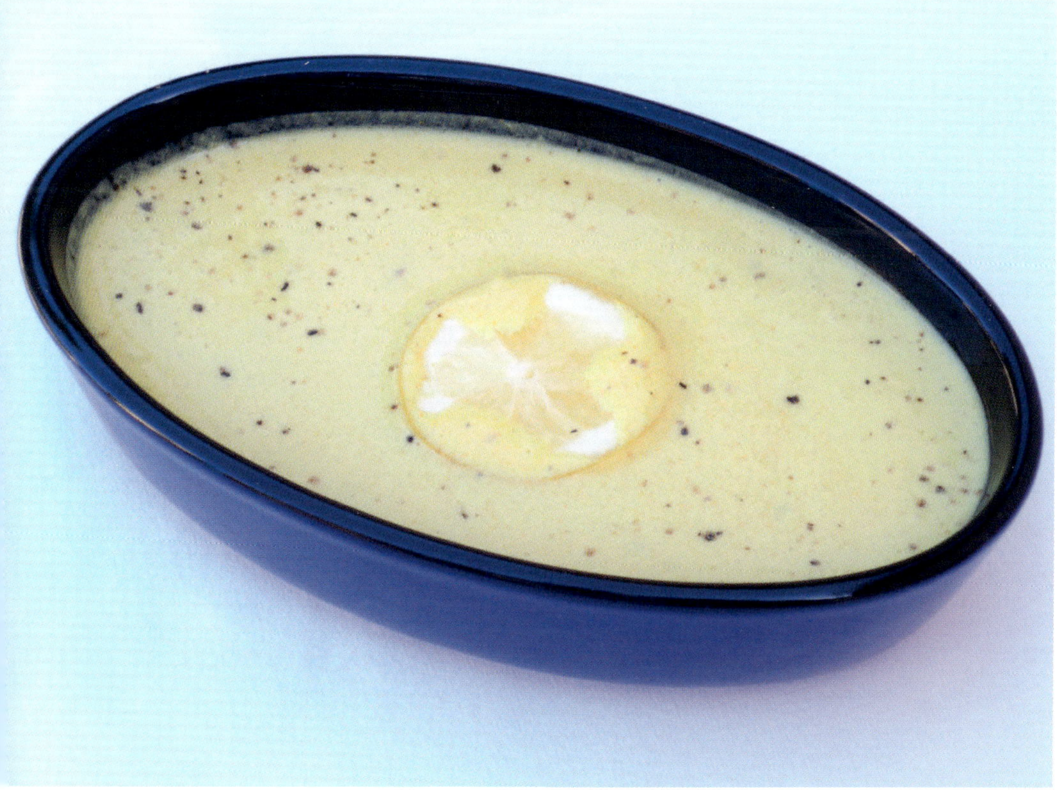

## Dressing for Salmon

**Ingredients:**

**2 tablespoons white wine vinegar**
**50g pickled onions**
**175g cool butter**
**4 tablespoons dry white wine**
**2 tablespoons double cream**
**6 tablespoons water or fish stock**

Method:

Chop the pickled onions finely and put into a small pan together with the vinegar, wine and water or fish stock, bring to the boil and simmer until most of the liquid has evaporated, leaving just a little.

Add the cream and simmer until slightly thickened. Remove from the heat and having diced the butter, add this a little bit at a time and whisk to make a smooth sauce.

Pour the dressing over the cooked salmon just before serving.


## Avocado Sauce
ideal with cold salmon or raw vegetables

**Ingredients:**

**1 avocado**
**1 clove garlic**
**1 tablespoon lemon juice**
**15fl oz/150ml Greek yoghurt**
**Salt and black pepper**

Method:

Spoon out the avocado from the skin and put into a bowl. Mash it into a puree together with the lemon juice, crushed garlic, seasoning and Greek yoghurt, mixing combining until you have a pale green creamy sauce.

Cover the bowl with cling film. This stops the avocado discolouring.

Put into the fridge until you need it later in the day.

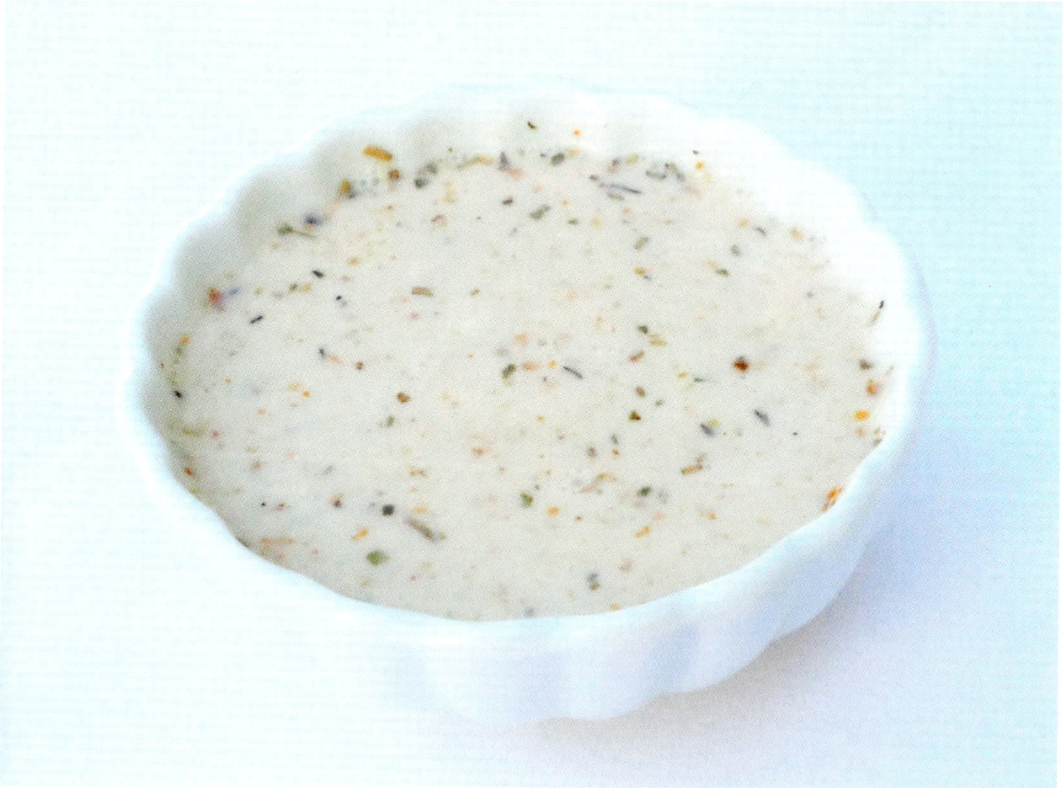

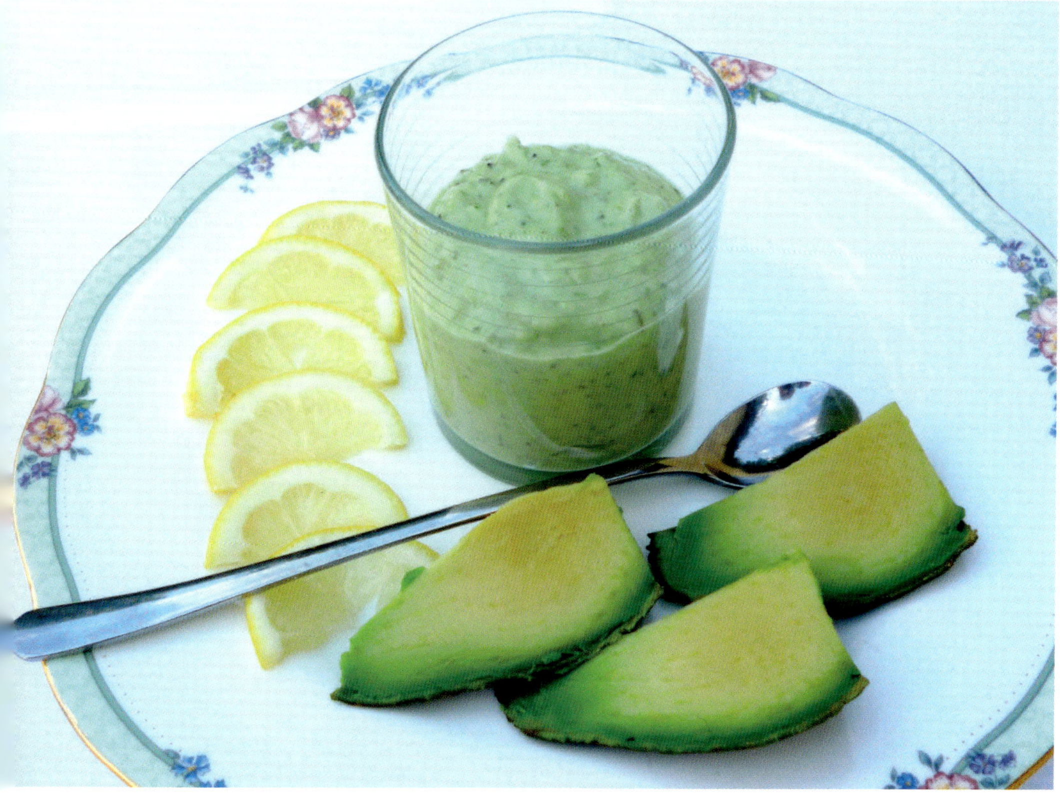

## Herb Butter Sauce
ideal with fish, hot carrots, potatoes, or chops

**Ingredients:**

**Method:**

**1 tablespoon chopped chives**

**175g soft butter**

**1 teaspoon chopped tarragon**

**4 tablespoons chopped curled leaf parsley**

**1 clove garlic**

**1 teaspoons lemon juice**

**Salt and black pepper**

Crush the garlic and mix all the ingredients together. Liquidize or blitz if preferred.

Cover and store in the fridge in little portions ready to serve.

## Potato and Wine Sauce
for white fish

**Ingredients:**

**Method:**

**2 medium potatoes**

**1 small onion**

**3 tablespoons olive oil**

**2 tablespoons apple cider vinegar**

**1 tablespoon white wine**

**Pinch of salt and pepper**

**Chopped curled leaf parsley to decorate**

Dice the onion, cut the potatoes in half and boil together until soft.

Mash these and mix in the other ingredients but NOT the chopped parsley.

When serving with the fish add a sprinkle of parsley to decorate.

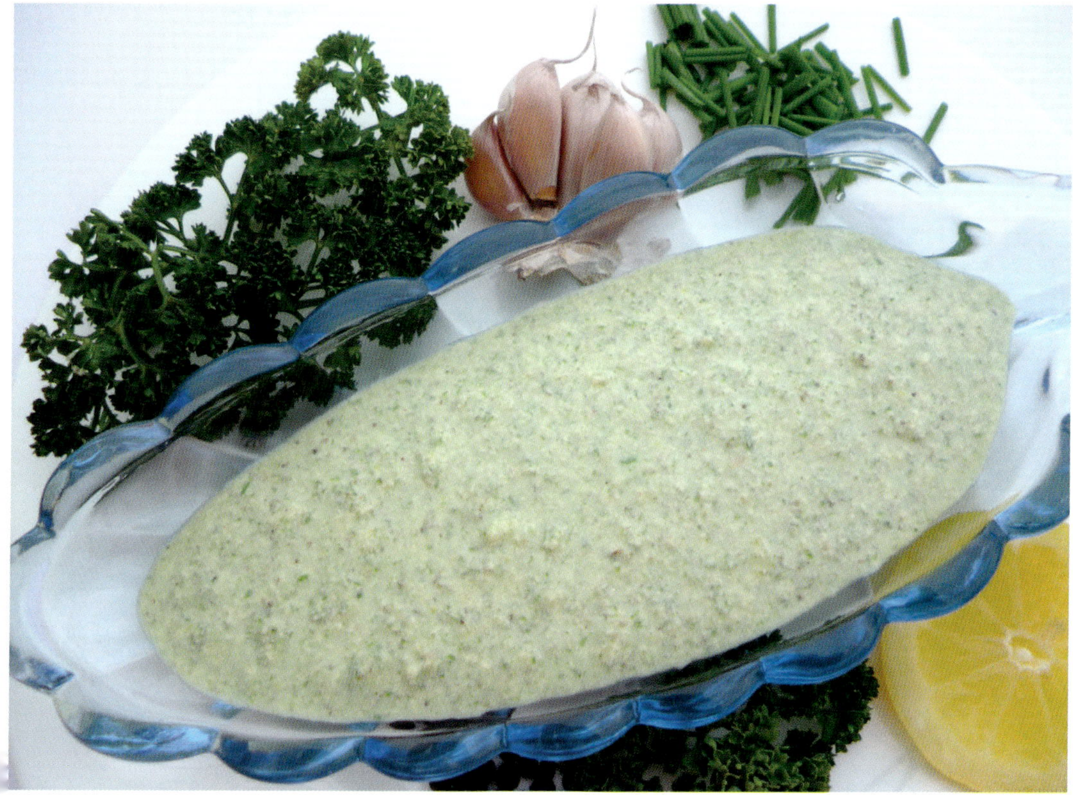

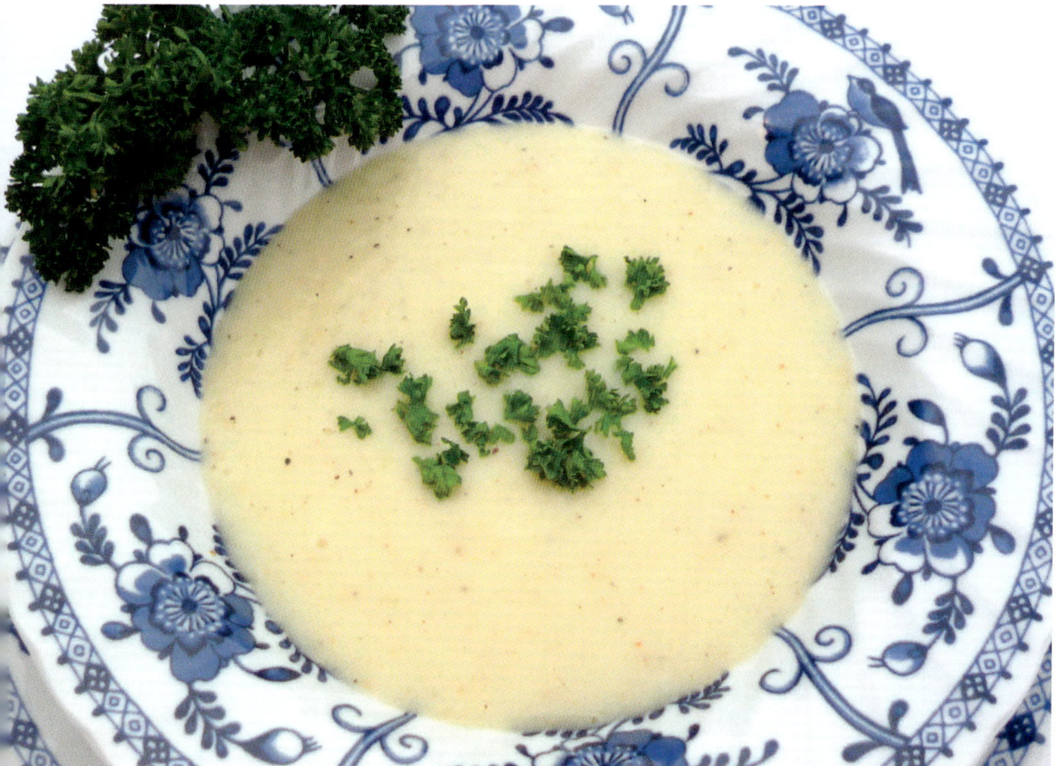

# White Wine Cream
for salmon

**Ingredients:**

**Half onion, finely chopped**
**1 tablespoon olive oil**
**2 cloves garlic, finely chopped**
**1 glass white wine**

**2 tablespoons single cream**
**1 tablespoon of basil pesto**
**Lemon slices and fresh dill to garnish**

Method:

Put the finely chopped onion into a frying pan with the oil and cook until softened.

Add the garlic and cook for 1 - 2 minutes but take care not to brown.

Add the wine and bubble for a minute or until it begins to evaporate.

Stir in the single cream thoroughly and remove from heat and stir in the pesto.

You can pour this over your cooked salmon, placing the slices of lemon and fresh dill on top ready to serve with vegetables.

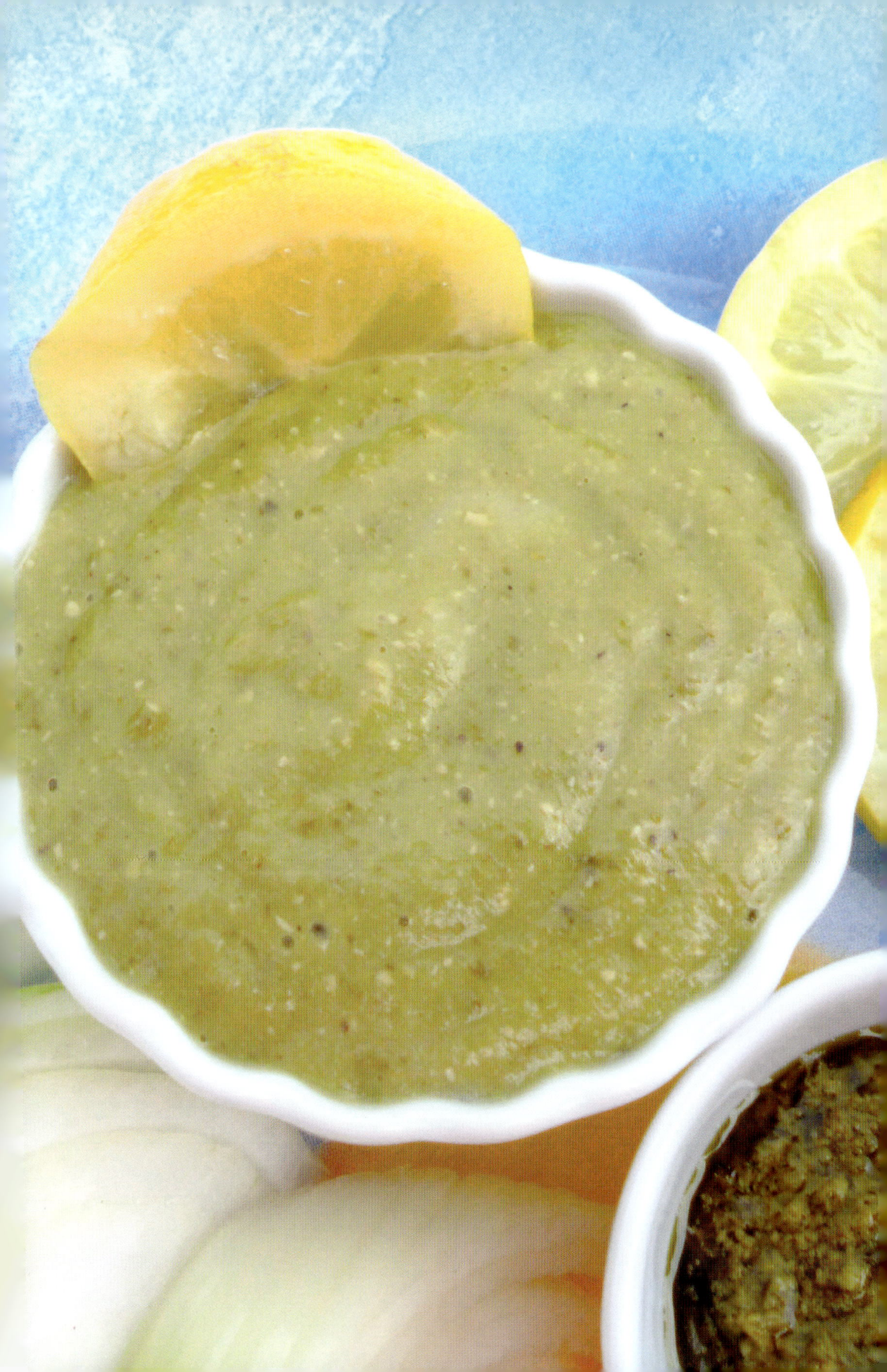

# ~ Meat ~

## Medium Hot Dry Pepper Mix
for stir-fry with pork

**Ingredients:**

**1 red onion**
**2 cloves garlic**
**Half teaspoon of dry basil**
**Half teaspoon of dry oregano**
**Pinch of cumin**
**1 red and 1 green bell peppers**
**Pinch salt (if required)**
**Small pinch of dried chillies**

**Method:**

Finely chop the red onion and chop the red and green peppers.

Crush the garlic and mix all the ingredients together. Liquidize or blitz if preferred.

Cover and store in the fridge in little portions ready to add to the stir-fry or pork before cooking in the oven.


## Fresh Mint Sauce
for lamb

**Ingredients:**

**10 fresh mint leaves**
**1 tablespoon brown sugar**
**2 teaspoon liquid honey**
**10fl oz/300ml apple cider vinegar**
**A little water if necessary**

**Method:**

Wash and dry mint and chop finely then blend all the ingredients together.

Place in the fridge for 2 to 3 hours and serve cold.

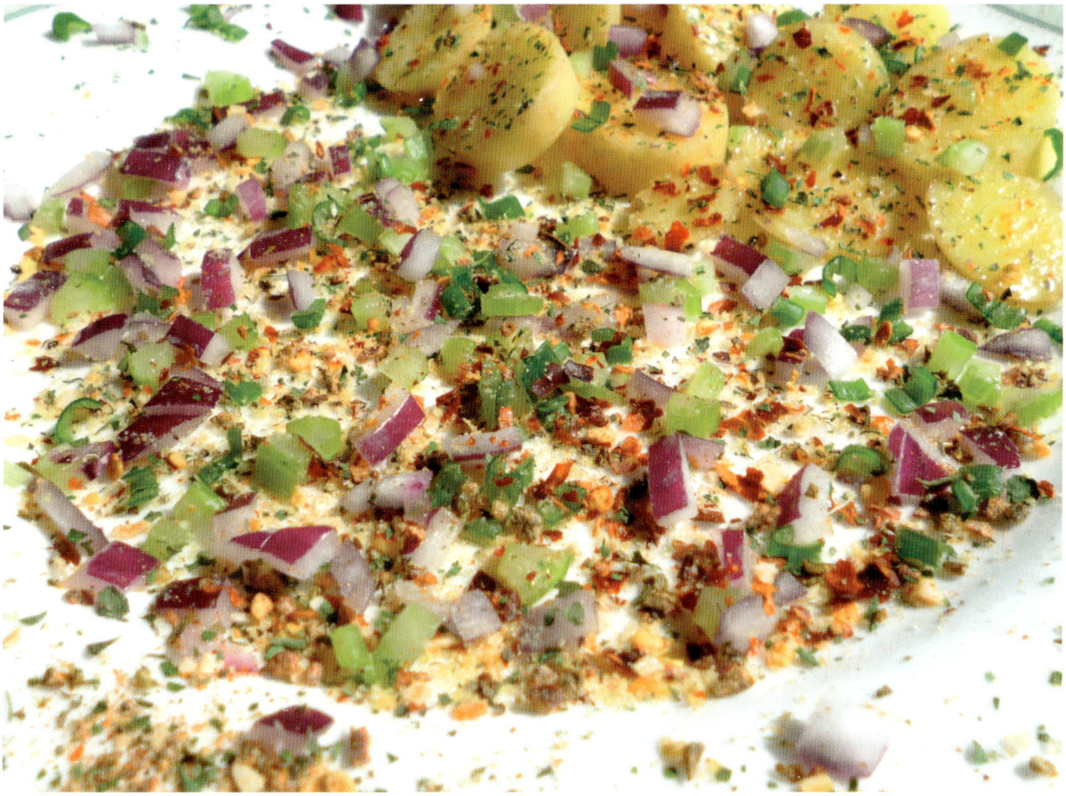

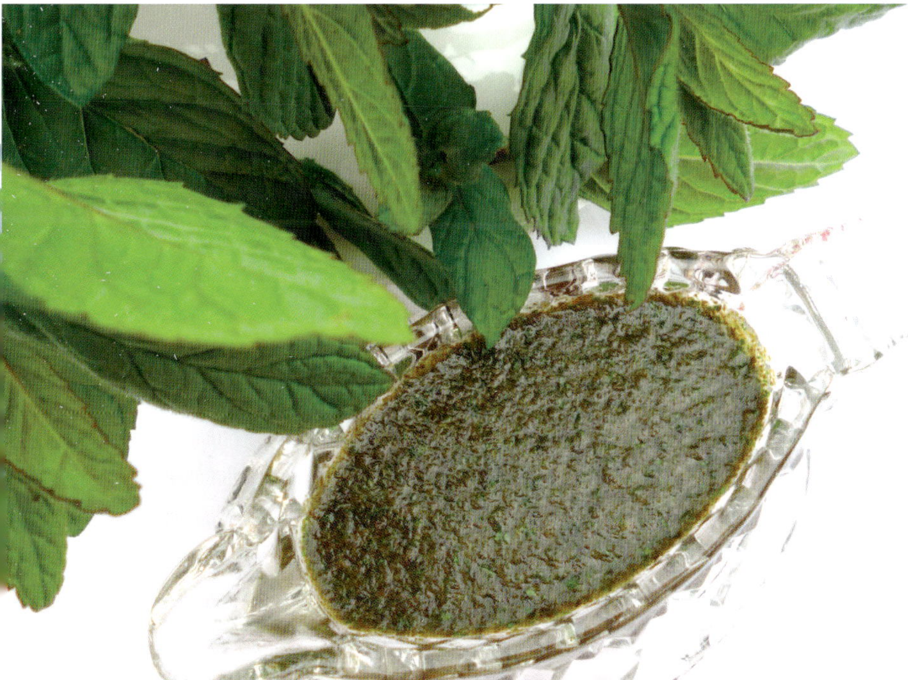

## Tasty Curry and Honey Sauce
for diced pork

**Ingredients:**

**Half a teaspoon curry powder**
**Quarter teaspoon cayenne pepper**
**1 tablespoon honey**
**20fl oz/600ml apple cider vinegar**
**Half a teaspoon salt**
**1 tablespoon plain flour**
**12 cloves (remove during cooking)**

Method:

Mix flour, curry powder and cayenne pepper with a little water.

Add the other ingredients and bring to the boil, turn down the heat and gentle simmer for 15 minutes, stirring to avoid burning.

## Homemade Tomato Sauce

**Ingredients:**

**1500g red tomatoes**
**50g shallots or onions**
**2 teaspoon French mustard**
**1 tablespoon olive oil**
**Pinch of cayenne pepper**
**1 teaspoon paprika**
**1 teaspoon salt**
**1 teaspoon crushed garlic**
**4g caster sugar**
**20fl oz/600ml apple cider vinegar**

Method:

Put chopped shallots/onions, crushed garlic and oil into a saucepan and cook until softened.

Add cut tomatoes and all the remaining ingredients and simmer gentle for 40 minutes remove from heat, blend and blitz with electric mixer and return to the heat and cook for a further 10 minutes stirring all the time.

When cold pour into an air-tight bottle or container and store in a dry place.

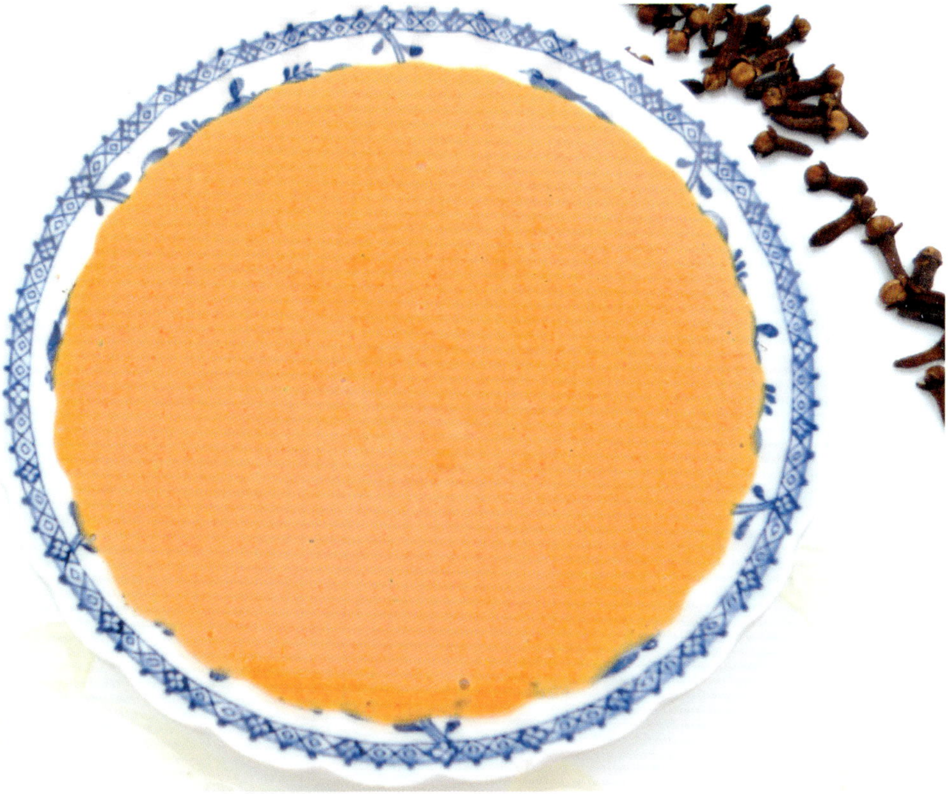

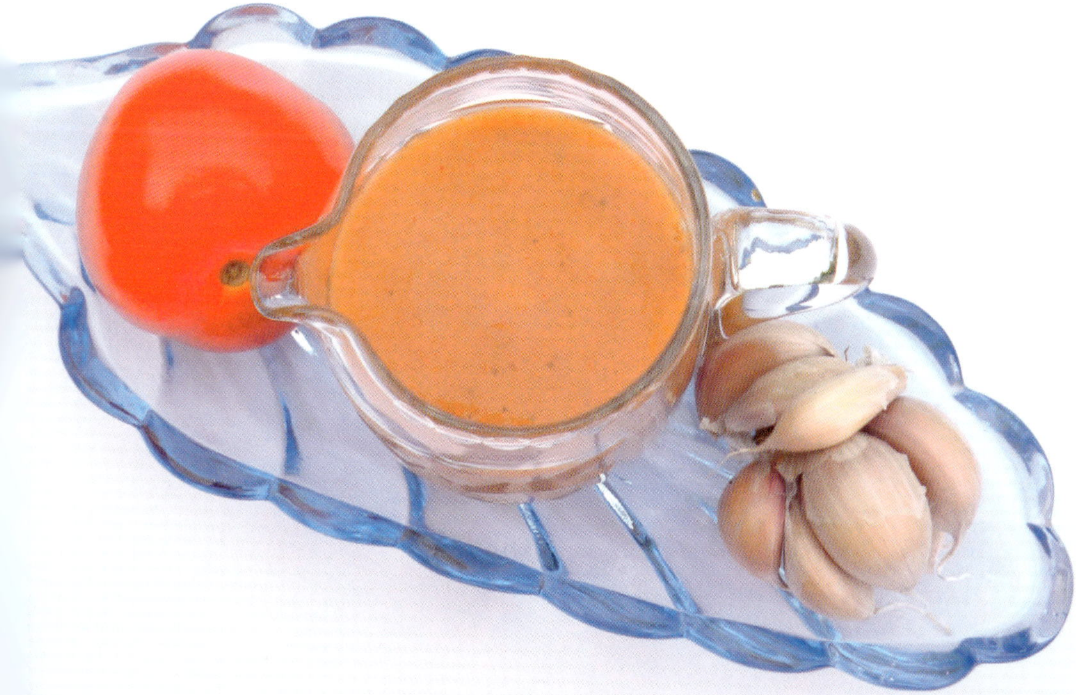

## Sweet and Sour Sauce

**Ingredients:**

**3 dessertspoon sugar**
**1 dessertspoon cornflour**
**1 dessertspoon soy sauce**
**4 dessertspoon wine vinegar**
**1 dessertspoon tomato puree**
**Pinch salt**
**10fl oz/275ml water**
**1 small tin chopped/ diced pineapple**
**4 pickled onions or 1 onion finely chopped**

**Method:**

Place sugar, corn flour, soy sauce, vinegar, tomato puree and salt into a bowl and mix together.

Pour into a saucepan add the chopped pineapple and chopped onion and cook until sauce thickens, stirring all the time for approximately 1min 30 seconds.

## Apple Sauce
for pork, goose or duck

**Ingredients:**

**500g apples**
**4 tablespoons water**
**40g butter or margarine**
**Cupful of sugar**

**Method:**

Peel, core and chop apples.

Place in a covered saucepan with water and sugar and cook over a low heat until pulpy.

Pour into a mixer, add the butter/margarine and blend until smooth.

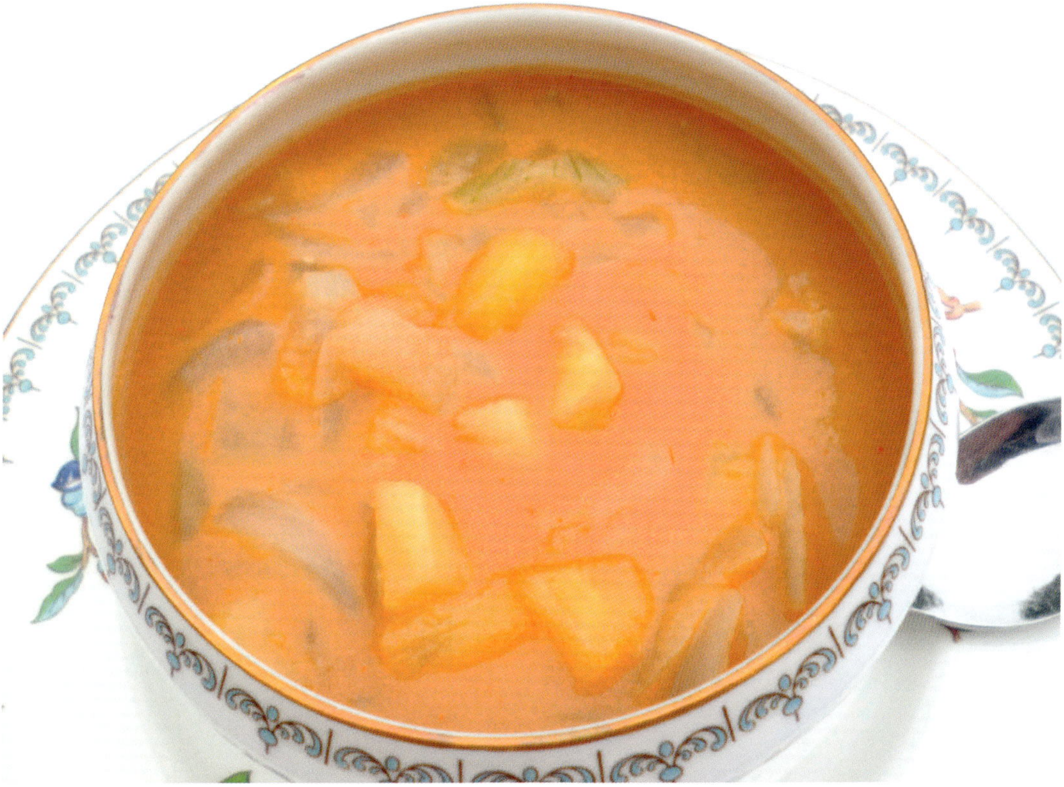

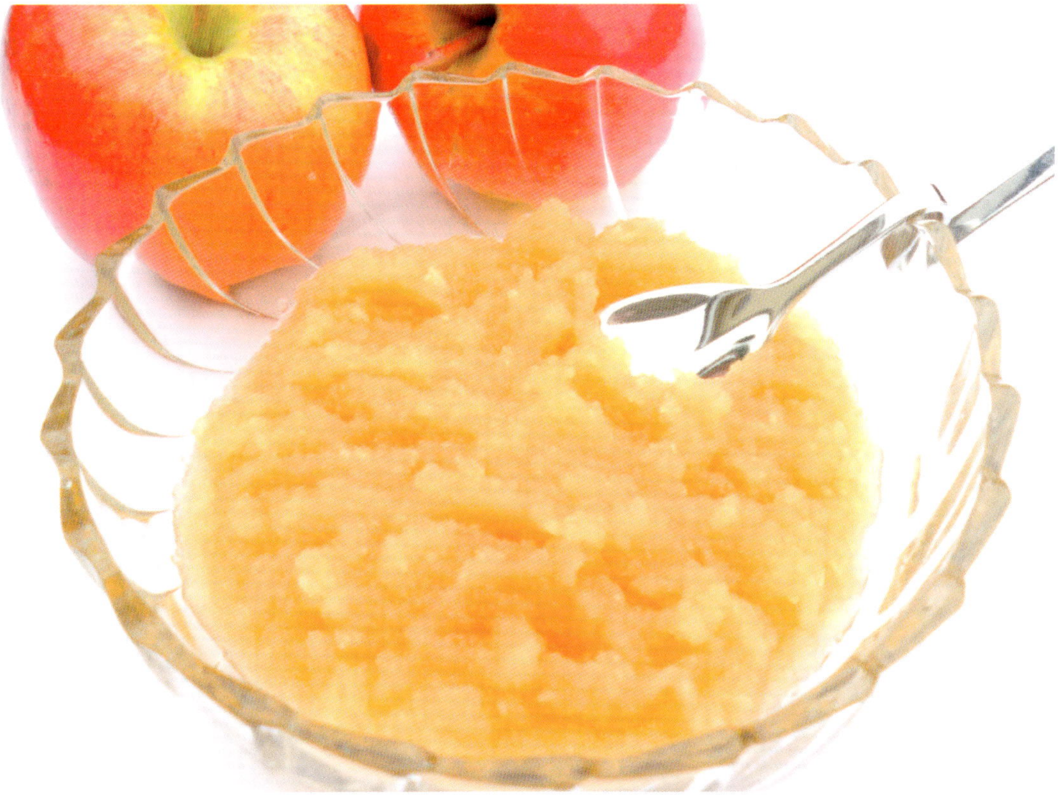

## Redcurrant and Ginger Sauce
for gammon, tongue or ham

**Ingredients:**

**4 tablespoons redcurrant jelly (high fruit)**
**4 tablespoons port**
**1 lemon**
**1 orange**
**1 teaspoon of dry mustard powder**
**1 teaspoon ground ginger**

Method:

Scrape the peel from the lemon and the orange, then cut into small strips. Boil in water for 5 minutes, then drain.

Place the redcurrant jelly in a pan with the port, whisking them together on a low heat for 5 to 10 minutes.

The redcurrant jelly will not melt completely so you can sieve it to get rid or any little pieces.

In a bowl mix the mustard and ginger with the juice of half the lemon, then add the juice of 1 orange, the port and redcurrant mixture and add the strips of orange and lemon peel.

Mix well and it is ready.

This sauce is best served cold.

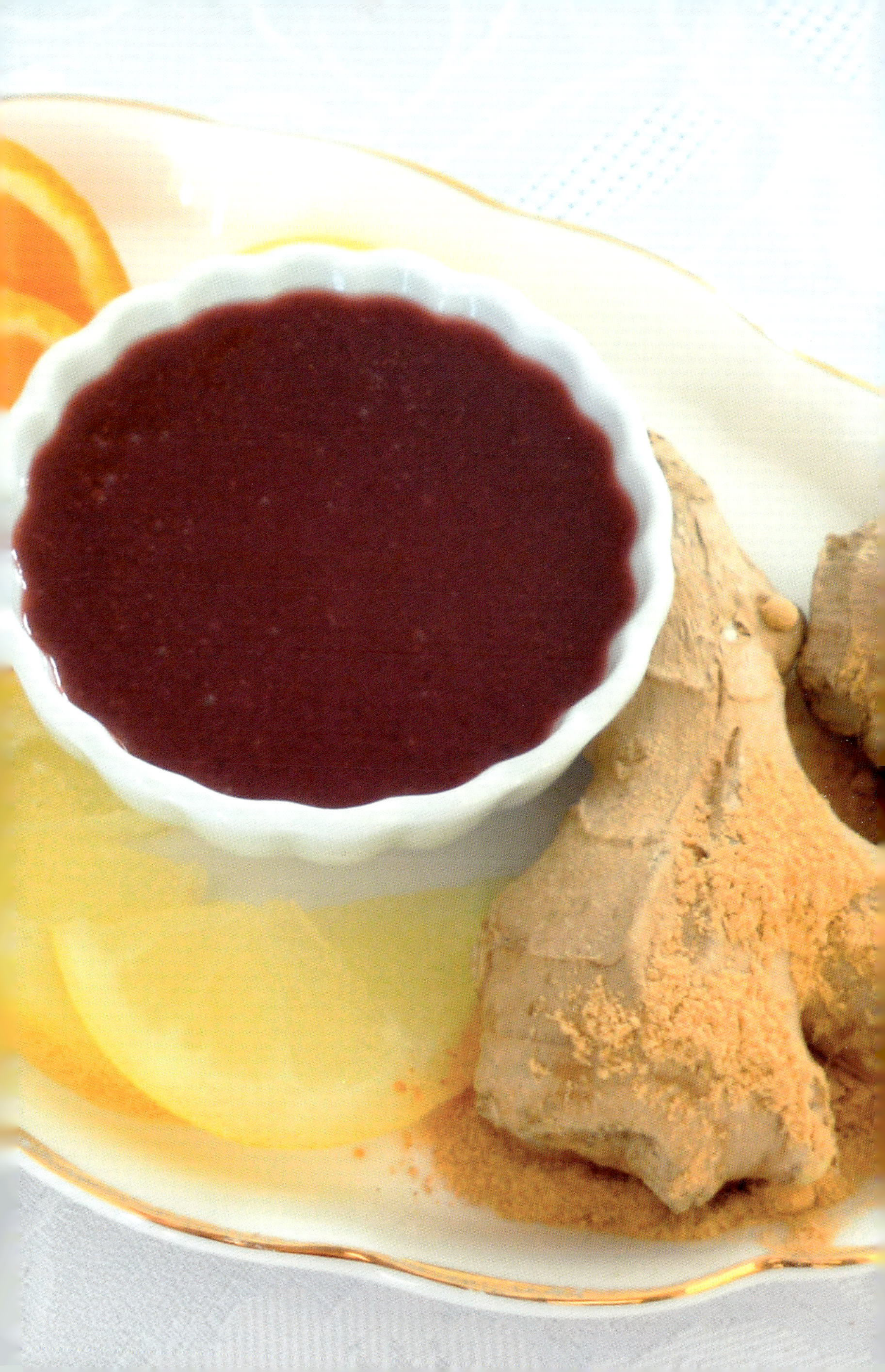

## Mushroom and Yoghurt Sauce

**Ingredients:**

**50g/2ozs butter**
**300g/10ozs finely chopped mushrooms**
**2 tablespoons yoghurt**
**Little marjoram**
**Pinch of oregano**
**Little grated nutmeg**
**Little chopped parsley**
**Salt and pepper to taste**

**Method:**

Put the chopped mushrooms, butter, parsley, herbs and seasoning into a pan and sauté for 8 to 10 minutes.

Add the yoghurt and simmer for 15 minutes until the yoghurt has been incorporated.

Do not let it boil or the yoghurt will separate.

Remove from the heat, stir well and serve.

## Homemade Horseradish Sauce

**Ingredients:**

**50g/2oz fresh horseradish**
**1 teaspoon sugar**
**1 cup of double cream**
**Half teaspoon mustard powder**
**Half teaspoon salt**
**Half teaspoon white pepper**
**2 teaspoons white wine vinegar**

**Method:**

Let the root of the horseradish soak in cold water for 1 hour then wash and scrape clean.

Grate the horseradish or cut very finely.

Whip the cream to soft peaks and fold in the horseradish, sugar, mustard, salt, pepper and vinegar.

Serve cold with beef.

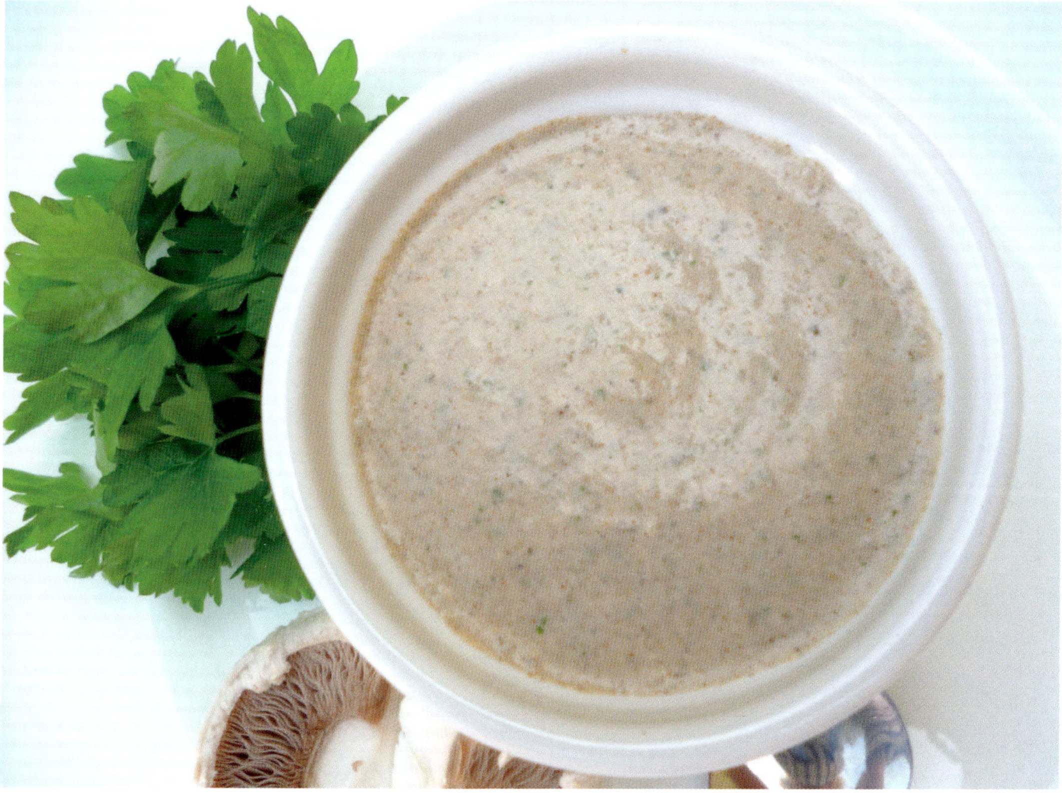

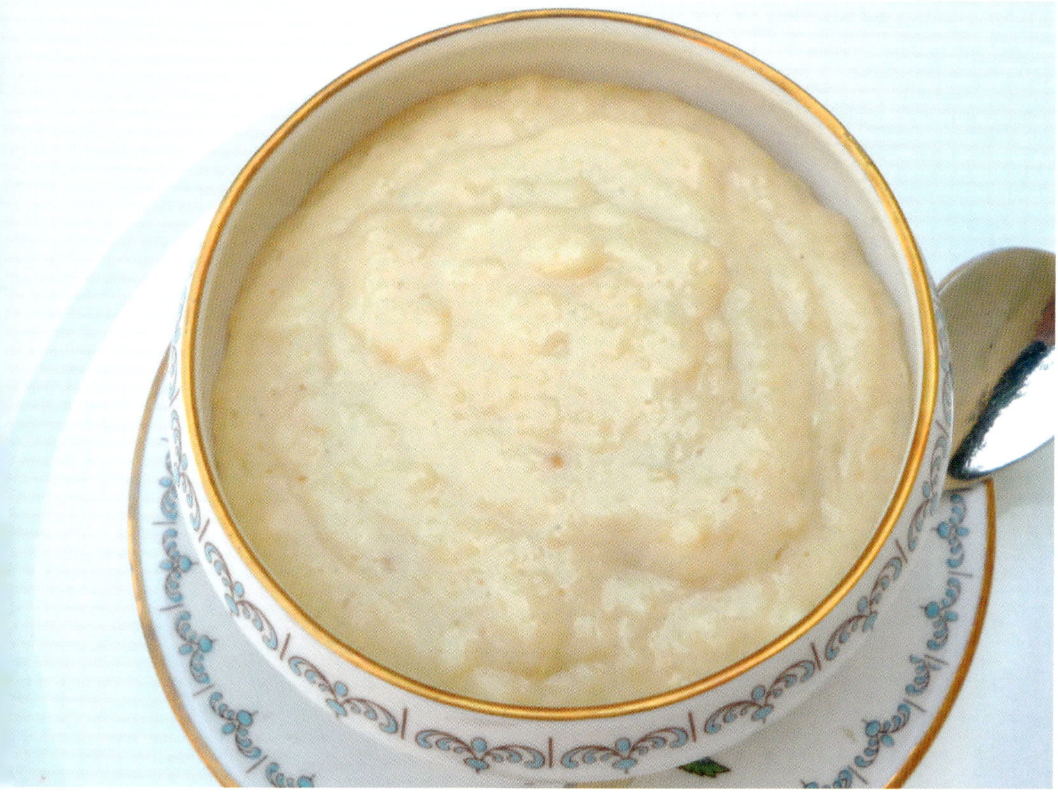

## Herb Butter
A finishing touch on steak or lamb chops

**Ingredients:**

**2 teaspoon of chopped thyme and flat leaf parsley mixed**

**50g/2oz butter**

**Method:**

Chop the thyme and parsley finely then mix together with the butter with a knife.

With your fingers make a sausage shape 2 -3 cm/1 inch thick, wrap in foil, roll between two boards to make an even sausage shape.

Place in the fridge so it is hard enough to cut into slices to place on the top of steak, chops or chicken pieces.

## A Simple Tomato Sauce
for baked aubergine and cheese

**Ingredients:**

**60ml/4 tablespoons olive oil**

**1 medium onion, finely chopped**

**1 clove garlic, finely chopped**

**450g/1lb tomatoes, fresh or tinned, chopped with their juice**

**Salt and black pepper**

**A few leaves of fresh basil or sprigs of flat leaf parsley**

**Method:**

Heat the oil in a medium saucepan.

Add the onion, cook over moderate heat until it is translucent, 5-8 minutes.

Stir in the garlic and tinned tomatoes, (add 45ml/3 tablespoons water if you are using fresh tomatoes).

Add salt and pepper and the basil or parsley.

Cook for 20 - 30 minutes.

Pureé in a food processor ready to add to your dish.

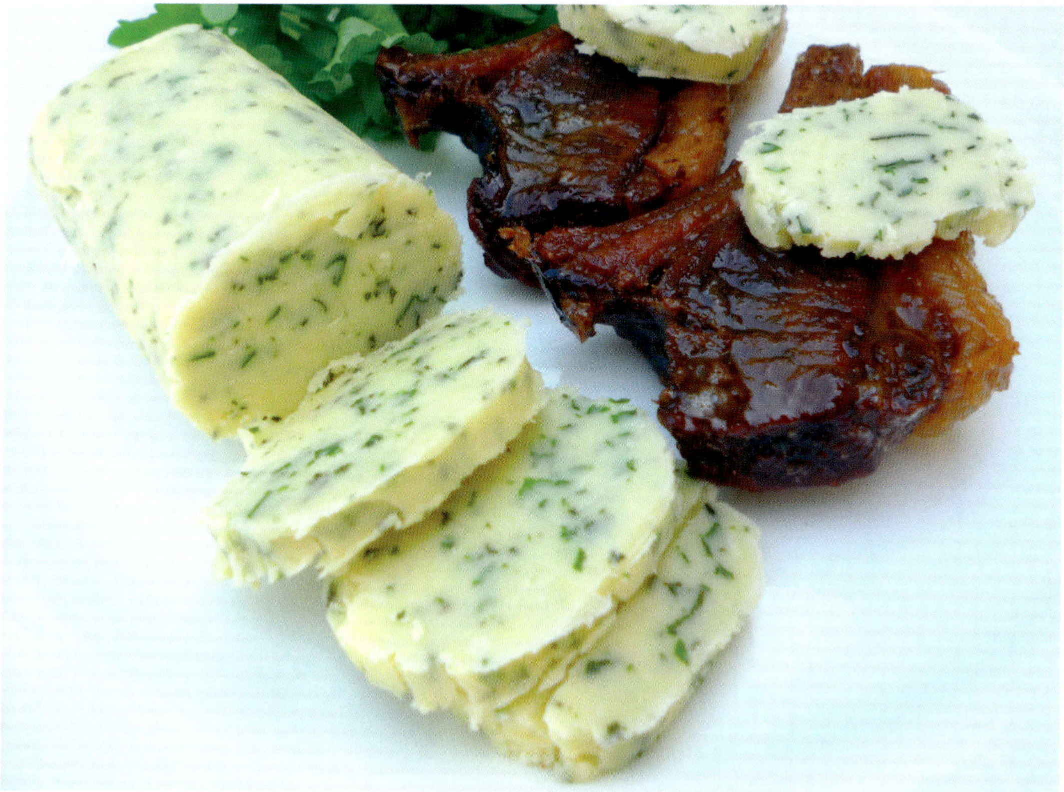

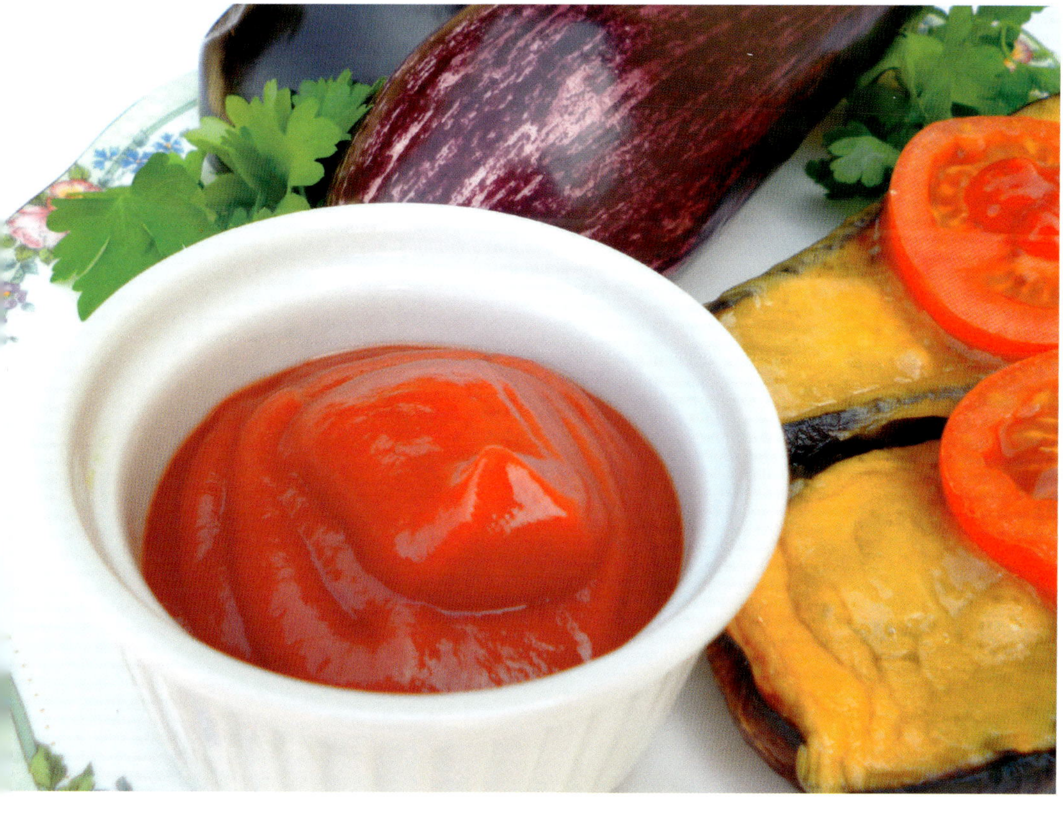

## An Oriental Sauce
for cubed chuck steak, rump or fillet steak

**Ingredients:**

1 teaspoon ground ginger
1 teaspoon minced garlic
1 teaspoon ground gloves
pinch ground nutmeg
pinch black pepper
2 onions, chopped
2 tablespoons groundnut oil

1 teaspoon salt
1 tablespoon brown sugar
2 tablespoons dark soy sauce
Juice of half a lemon
8fl oz/228ml water
6oz/170g sliced mushrooms
1 green pepper, seeded and sliced
1 tablespoon of red wine

Method:

Put the onions and oil in a saucepan and fry until soft, add the garlic, ginger, cloves, nutmeg and pepper and stir for 3 minutes.

Add the cubed steak and fry until browned on all sides.

Add the water, stir in the salt, sugar, soy sauce, lemon juice, add a little more water if necessary.

Bring to the boil, then cover and simmer for one and a quarter hours.

Add the mushrooms, peppers and wine and cook for a further 15 minutes or until meat is tender.

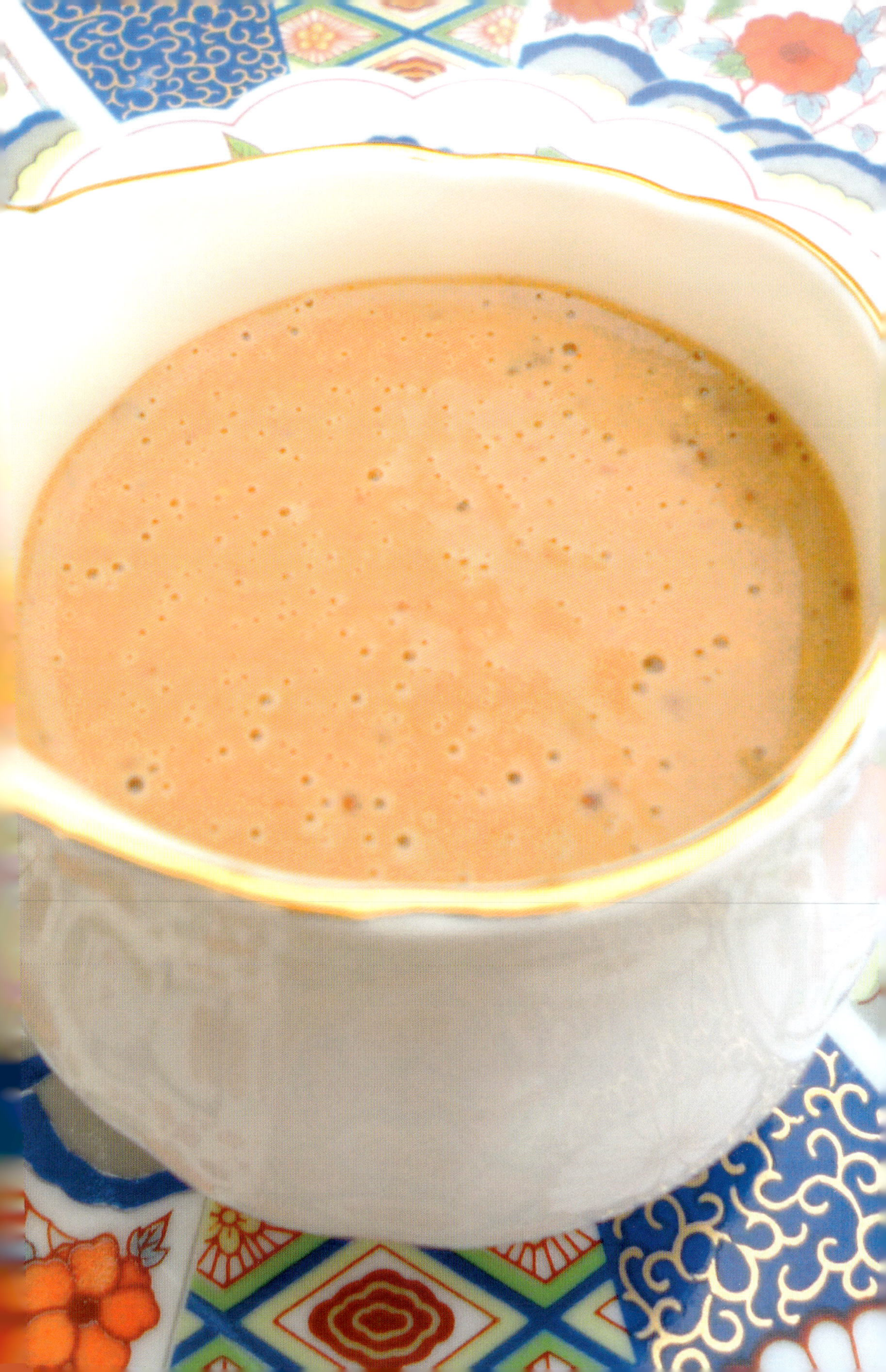

## Cucumber and Yoghurt Mixture
for curries

**Ingredients:**

**Half a cucumber**
**150g/5oz natural yoghurt**
**A little paprika**

Method:

Grate the cucumber and drain off any juice.

Mix with the yoghurt and add salt to taste.

Put into a small serving bowl and sprinkle a little paprika on the top.

## Cool Tomato Relish
for Indian Curries or any spicy meal

**Ingredients:**

**1 tin of chopped tomatoes**
**2 sticks of spring onions, finely chopped**
**Half teaspoon caster sugar**
**A little salt**
**3 tablespoons chopped fresh coriander**

Method:

Mix the chopped tomatoes, chopped spring onions, sugar, salt and chopped coriander together and blend to create a creamy mixture.

Serve at room temperature.

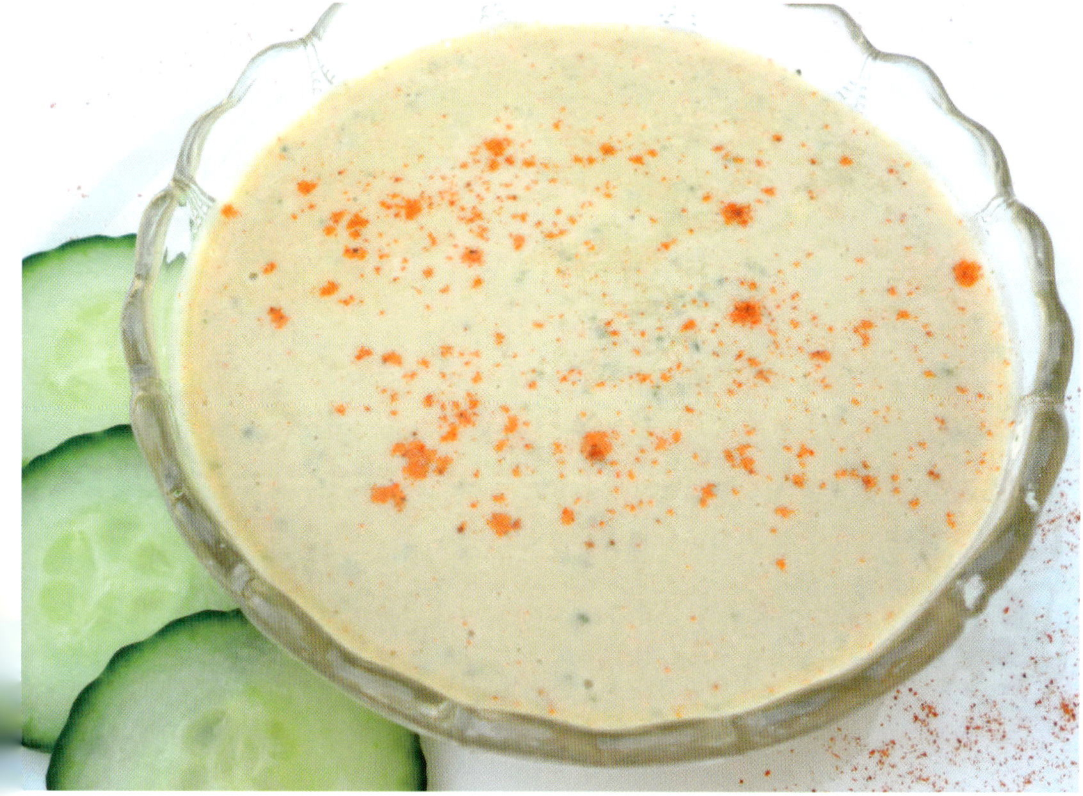

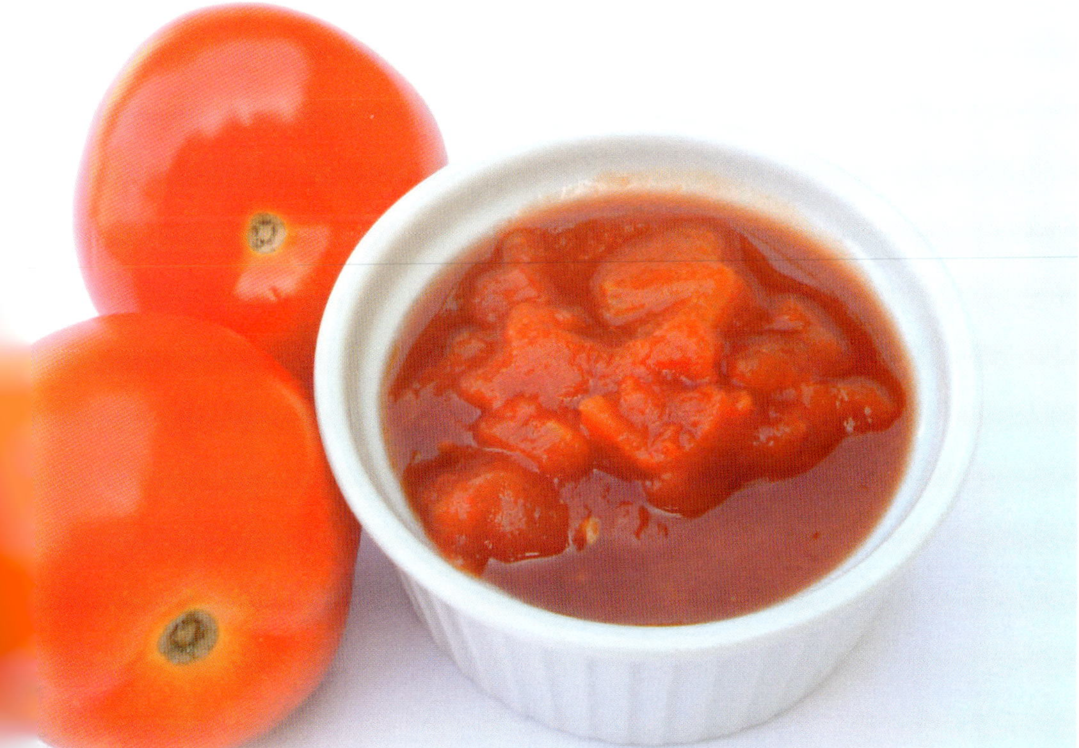

## Barbecue Sauce
for spare ribs, sausages and burgers

**Ingredients:**

2 tablespoons brown sugar
3 tablespoons sunflower oil
3 tablespoons white wine vinegar
3 tablespoons light soy sauce
3 tablespoons Worcester sauce

2 tablespoons sweet chilli sauce
1 tin chopped tomatoes
1 glove garlic (crushed)
1 teaspoon ground ginger
pinch of salt and pepper
1 teaspoon English mustard

Method:

Place all the ingredients together into a saucepan.

Bring to the boil stirring continuously until blended.

Remove from heat and let cool, then finally blitz the mixture a little ready to serve.

You can store this in the fridge for up to one month.

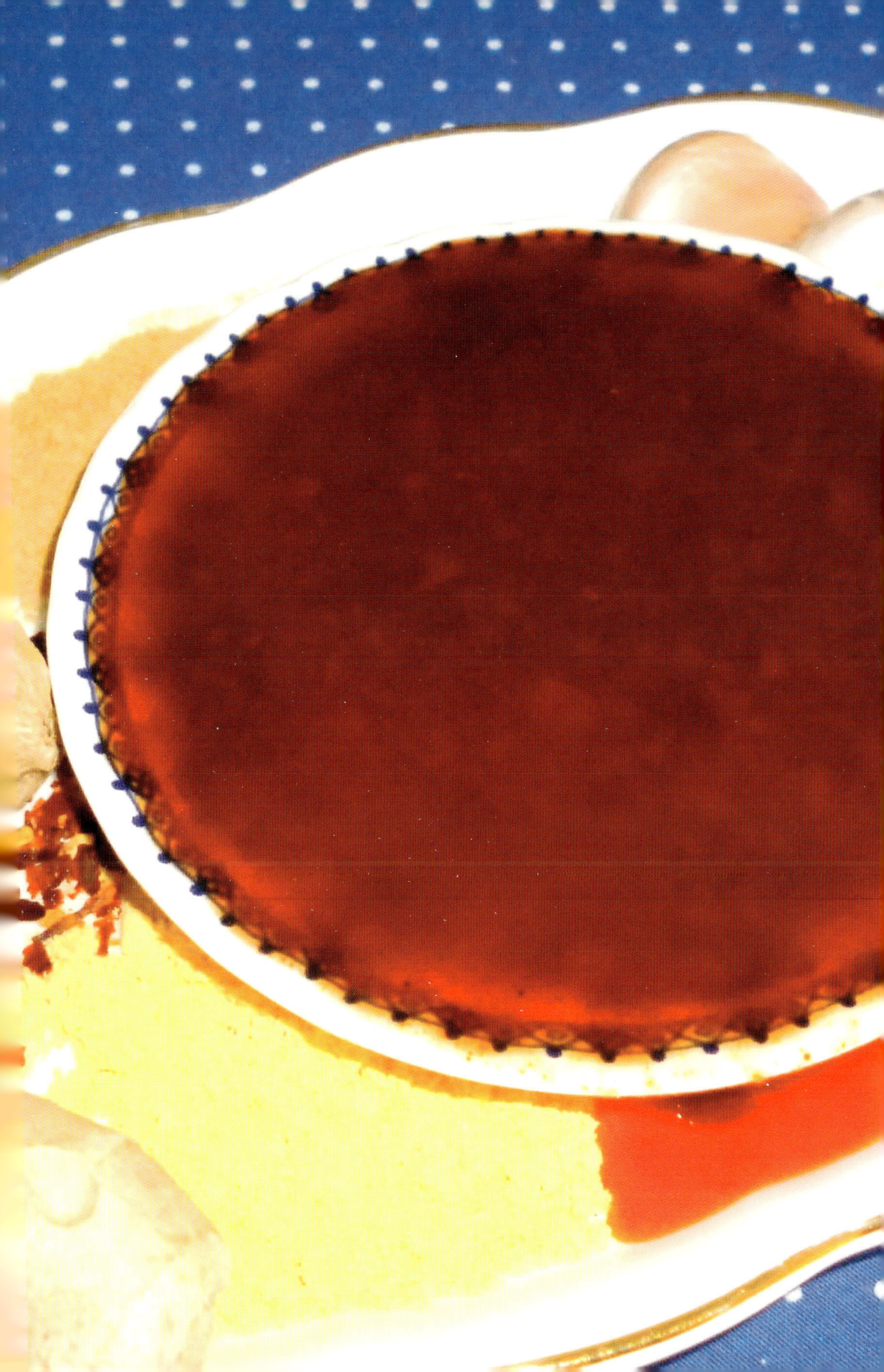

## Cold Cucumber Sauce
for all meat curries

**Ingredients:**

**Half a cucumber**
**1 tablespoon lemon juice**
**Half an onion, grated**
**Half a cup of single cream or low fat natural yoghurt**
**Salt and pepper to taste**
**2 teaspoons chopped fresh dill**
**Half a cup beef stock**

Method:

Peel and finely chop the cucumber.

Place the cucumber, lemon juice and onion in food processor. Process until smooth and fine.

Transfer the mixture to a bowl, stir in the cream or yoghurt, stock, salt and pepper to taste.

Add half the dill and stir until combined. Put into a serving dish, chill for 1 hour.

Sprinkle with remaining dill and serve.


## Lentil and Bacon Dressing
for beef instead of gravy

**Ingredients:**

**100g red lentils**
**2 cups beef stock**
**Half clove garlic, crushed**
**1 whole clove**
**1 bacon rasher, chopped**
**1 large tomato, chopped**
**Half an onion, chopped**
**Salt and pepper to taste**
**1 large potato, chopped**
**Juice of half a lemon**

Method:

Wash lentils and drain well. Place in a saucepan with stock, garlic, cloves, bacon, tomato, onion, salt and pepper.

Bring to the boil, reduce heat, simmer with lid on for 30 minutes.

Add chopped potatoes and simmer for a further 20 minutes. Remove from heat and allow to cool.

Blend in a blender or food processor. Add the lemon juice. Heat again before serving.

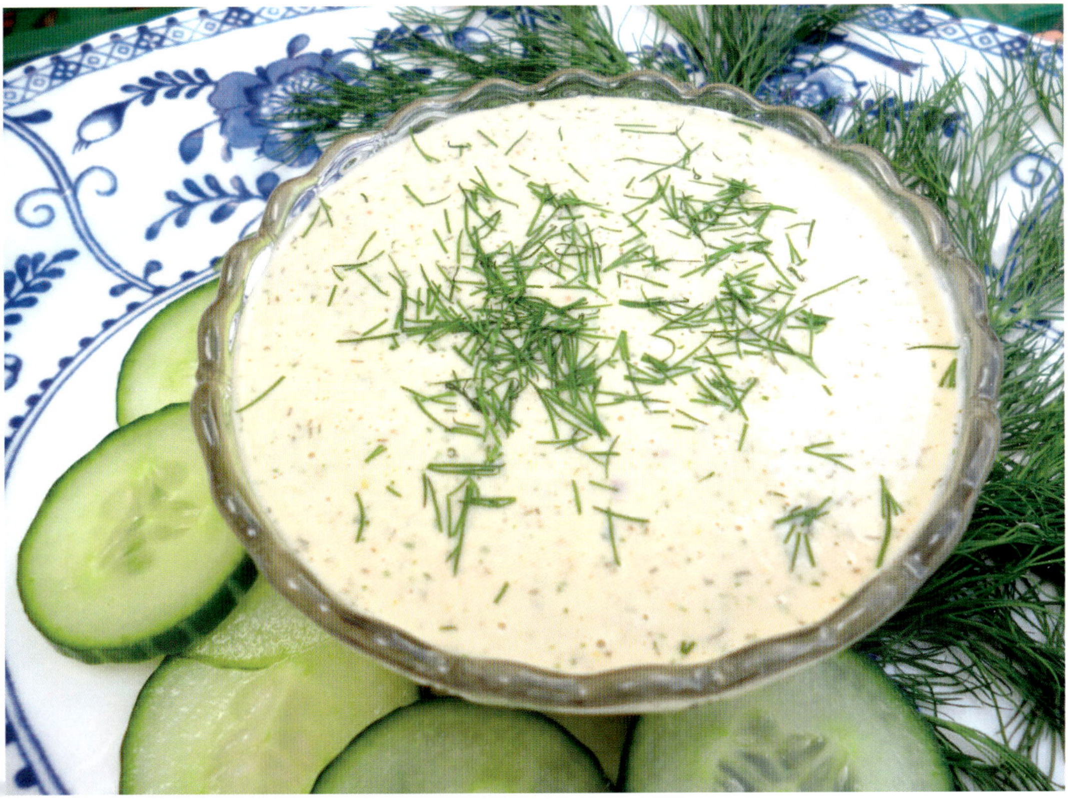

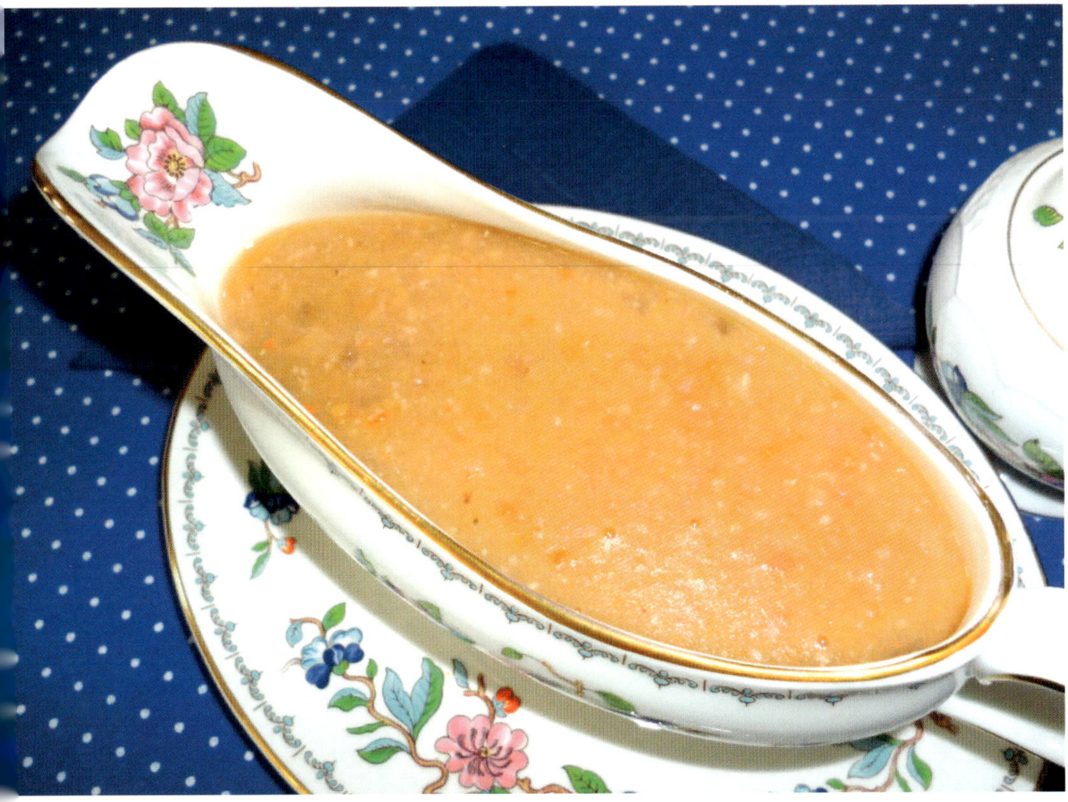

## Yorkshire Pudding Mixture
for beef

**Ingredients:**

**Half pint of milk**
**1 egg**
**4oz plain flour**
**Half teaspoon salt**
**2 cups of oil**

Method:

Mix the milk, egg, flour, salt together in a blender.

Heat the oil in an oven-proof dish in the oven and when very hot pour the batter mixture into the oil.

Cook for 30 minutes or until golden brown.

## A Spanish Sauce
for beef

**Ingredients:**

**3 rashers back bacon, chopped**
**4 tablespoons sunflower oil**
**1 large onion, chopped**
**2 tomatoes, chopped**
**3 medium mushrooms**
**1 teaspoon cornflour**
**1 carrot, finely chopped**
**1 cup beef stock**
**2 tablespoons sherry or dry red wine**

Method:

Fry the finely chopped bacon in the oil, add the chopped onion, carrot and mushrooms and stir until just turning brown.

Mix the cornflour with a little cold water. Add this to the mixture stirring into a smooth consistency, then add the chopped tomatoes, stock and sherry or dry red wine, if preferred.

Stir and simmer for ten minutes.

Strain, season to taste and use as required after re-heating.

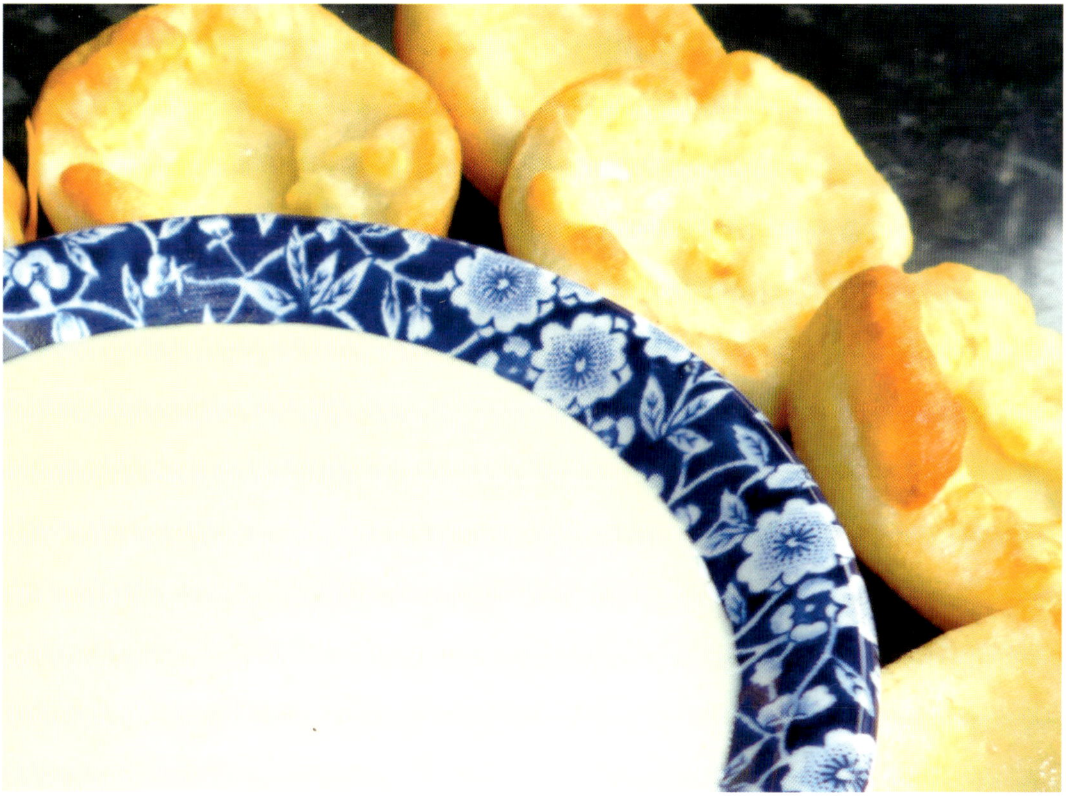

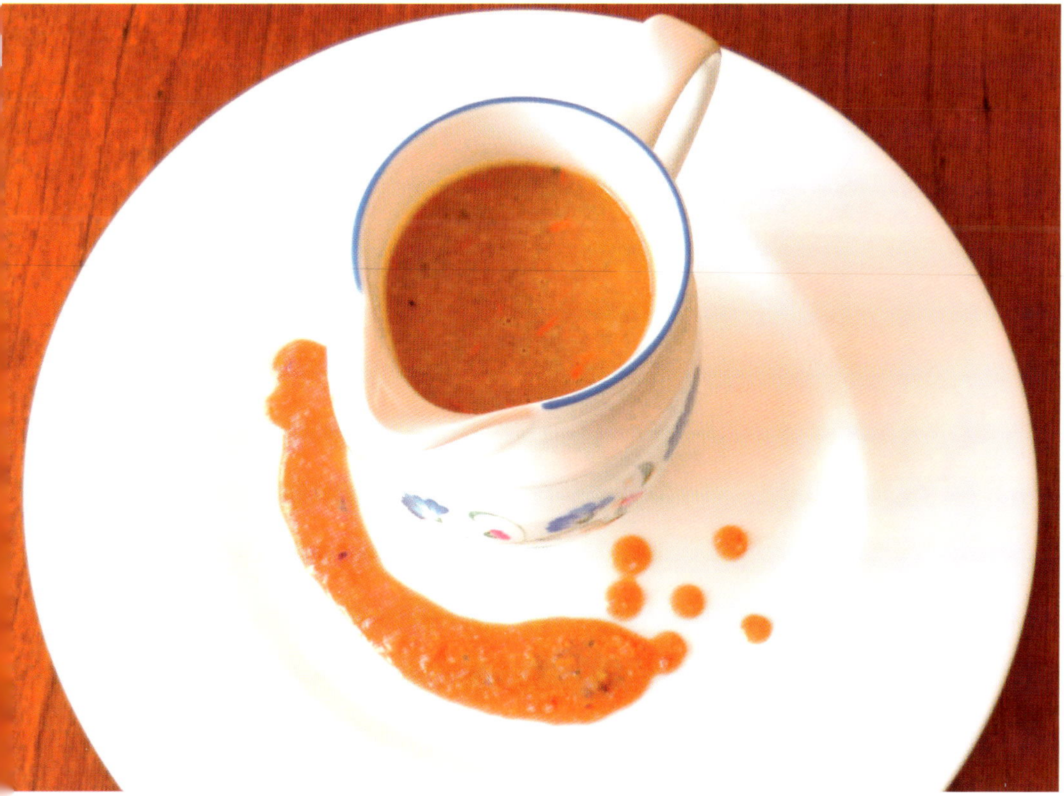

## Madeira Sauce

for hot ham, gammon or bacon

**Ingredients:**

**250ml medium white sauce (see medium white sauce recipe)**
**1 wineglass of stock**
**1 wineglass Madeira**
**Salt and pepper to taste**

**Method:**

Place the white sauce into a saucepan then stir in the stock.

Bring to the boil.

Stir in the Madeira little by little and when very hot season to taste and serve.

## Medium White Sauce

**Ingredients:**

**1oz butter**
**250ml hot milk**
**2oz plain plain flour**
**Salt and pepper to taste**

**Method:**

Melt the butter in a pan and add the flour stirring all the time with a wooden spoon, then add a little hot milk a drop at a time stirring continuously until the sauce is thick and creamy.

Bring to the boil stirring continuously to prevent lumps forming then season to taste.

Note: If lumps appear, strain it and add a small pat of butter before serving.

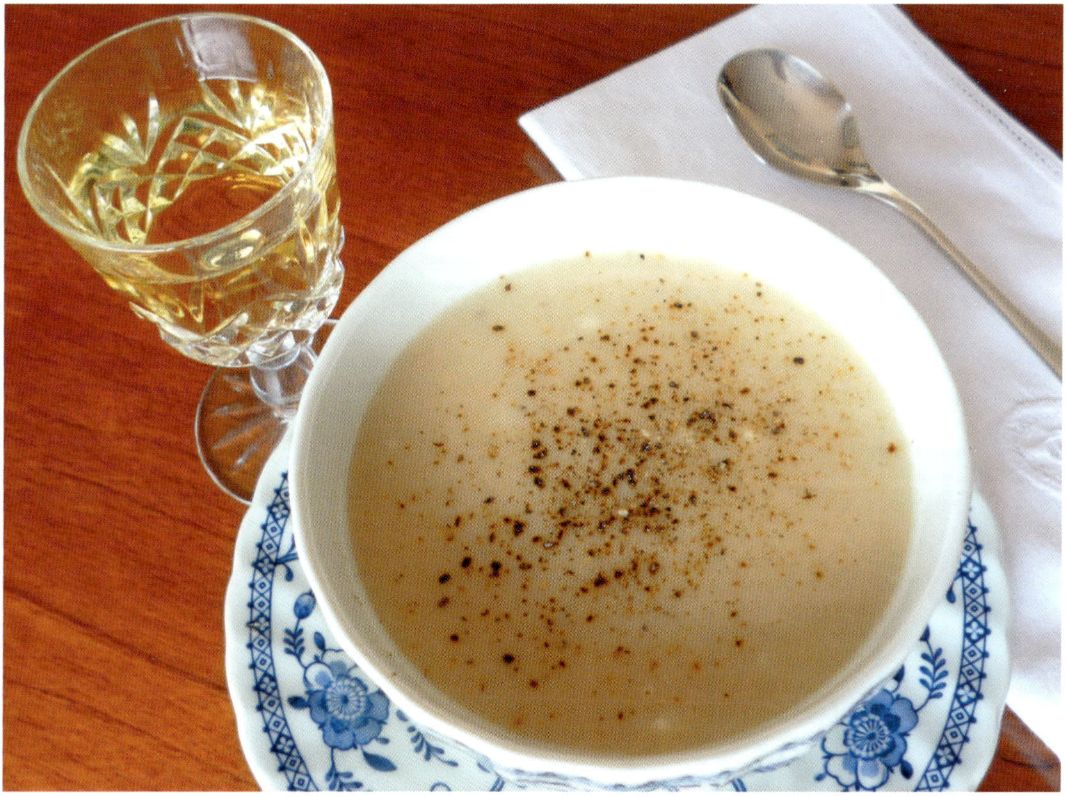

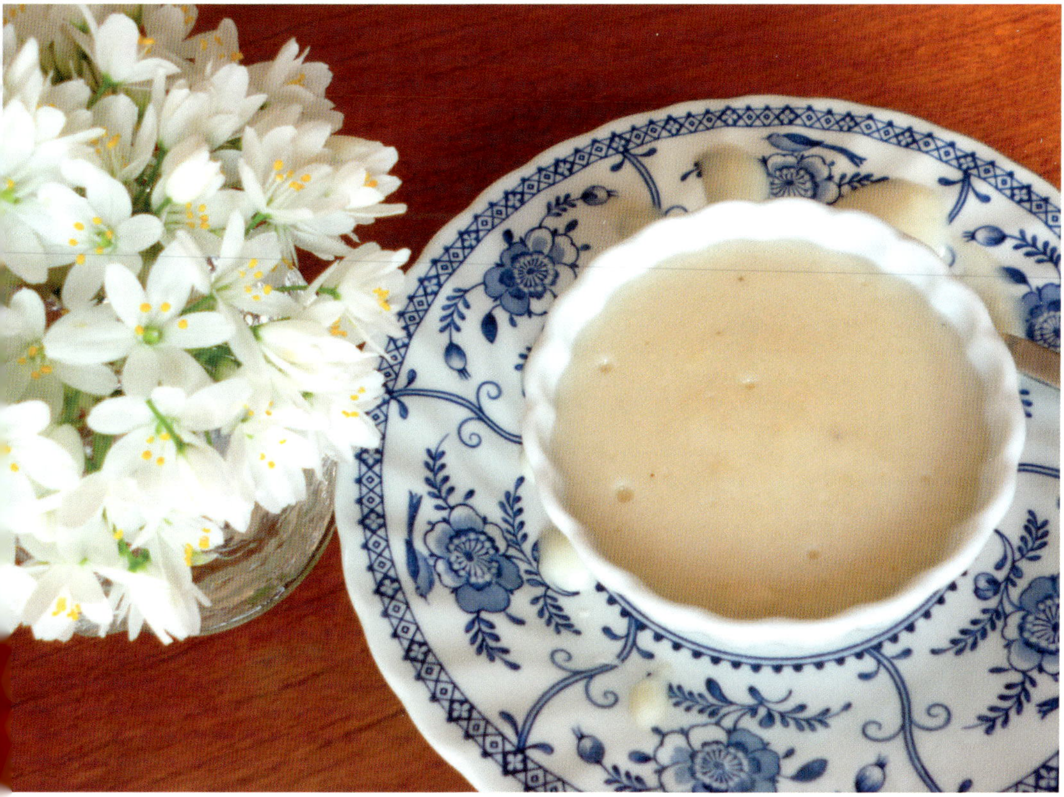

# ~ Poultry ~

## Celery Sauce
for pheasant or turkey

**Ingredients:**

**3 sticks of celery**
**1 chicken stock cube**
**1 tsp butter**
**1 tbs plain flour**
**Pinch of salt and pepper**
**300ml/10 fl oz milk**

Method:

Boil the celery in salted water or chicken stock until tender.

Then drain from water and blitz the celery then add the butter to the heated milk add flour slowly and stir well adding salt and pepper.

Stir altogether until creamy.

Use hot or cold with pheasant or turkey.

## Homemade Bread Sauce
for turkey, chicken or pheasant

**Ingredients:**

**75g bread**
**1 onion**
**10 cloves or use nutmeg if preferred**
**15fl oz/425ml milk**
**2 tablespoons double cream**
**50g butter or margarine**
**Pinch salt and pepper**

Method:

Use a liquidizer or prepare the breadcrumbs by hand.

Push the cloves into the onion and place in a saucepan with the milk.

Heat to boiling point and set aside for 30 minutes then remove the onion.

Just before serving re-heat and add breadcrumbs, seasoning and butter/margarine and stir for approximately 1 minute or until creamy. Then let stand for 15 minutes to allow the crumbs to swell and thicken the sauce.

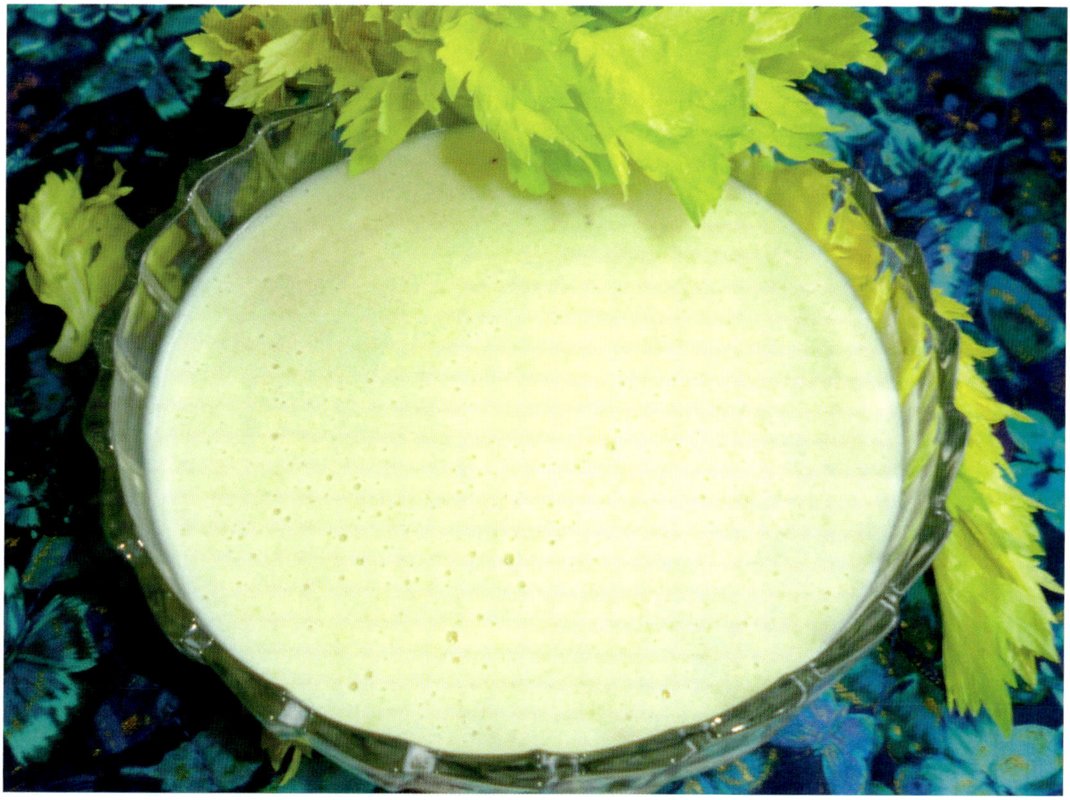

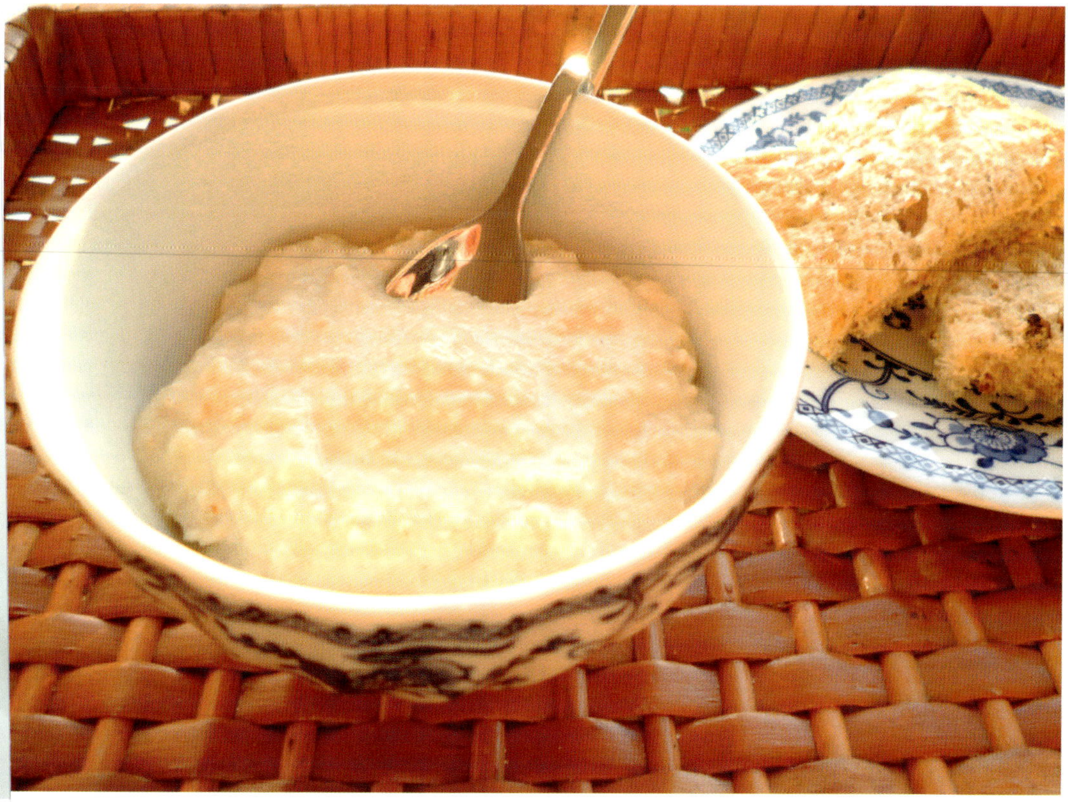

## Thyme and Parsley Balls
for pheasant or duck

**Ingredients:**

**1 small onion**
**100g/4oz fresh breadcrumbs**
**2 rashers of bacon**
**1 tablespoon olive oil**

**1 tablespoon chopped parsley**
**1 tablespoon chopped thyme**
**1 egg**
**1 lemon**
**Pinch of salt and pepper**

Method:

Chop the onion and bacon finely and lightly fry them together.

Make a bowl of breadcrumbs and add the olive oil, bacon, onion, finely chopped thyme, parsley, pepper, salt and juice of the lemon and a little grated rind.

Beat the egg for a short time and mix it into the mixture to bind it.

Dusting your hands with a little flour, roll the mixture into balls and place on a greased tin and put into the oven for 20 minutes at Gas mark 6 / 200°C / 400°F.

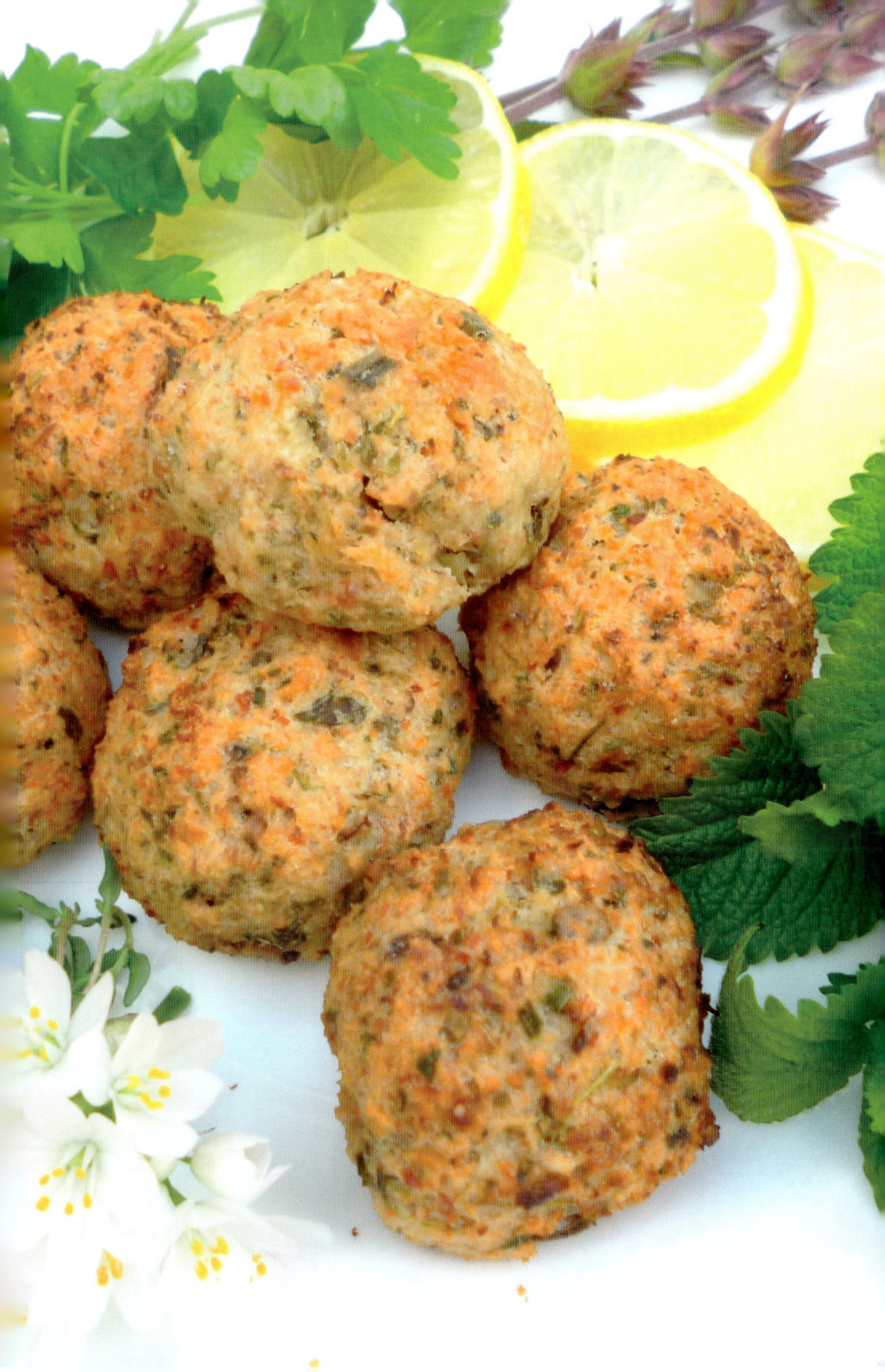

## Chilli dipping Sauce
for poultry kebabs

**Ingredients:**

**2 tablespoons desiccated coconut**
**4 tablespoons smooth peanut butter**
**Half a teaspoon chilli powder**
**2 teaspoons soy sauce**
**1 tablespoon light muscovite sugar**
**1 lime**

**Method:**

Grated zest and juice the lime.

Put all the ingredients including the coconut into a blender and whisk together then transfer into a small serving bowl ready for dipping.


## Creamy Orange Sauce
for duck or chicken

**Ingredients:**

**45ml/3 tablespoons brandy**
**300ml orange juice**
**3 spring onions, chopped**
**10ml/2 teaspoons cornflour**
**90ml/6 tablespoons low fat fromage frais**
**Small pinch salt and pepper**

**Method:**

Place the brandy, orange juice and chopped spring onions in a saucepan and bring to the boil.

Mix the cornflour with a little cold water then add the fromage frais and mix together. Add this to the mixture in the saucepan and stir over a moderate heat until blended together. Add the seasoning and pour the mixture over roast duck/chicken pieces and serve with boiled rice or pasta and/or green salad.

Note: the cornflour stabilises the fromage frais and helps prevent it curdling.

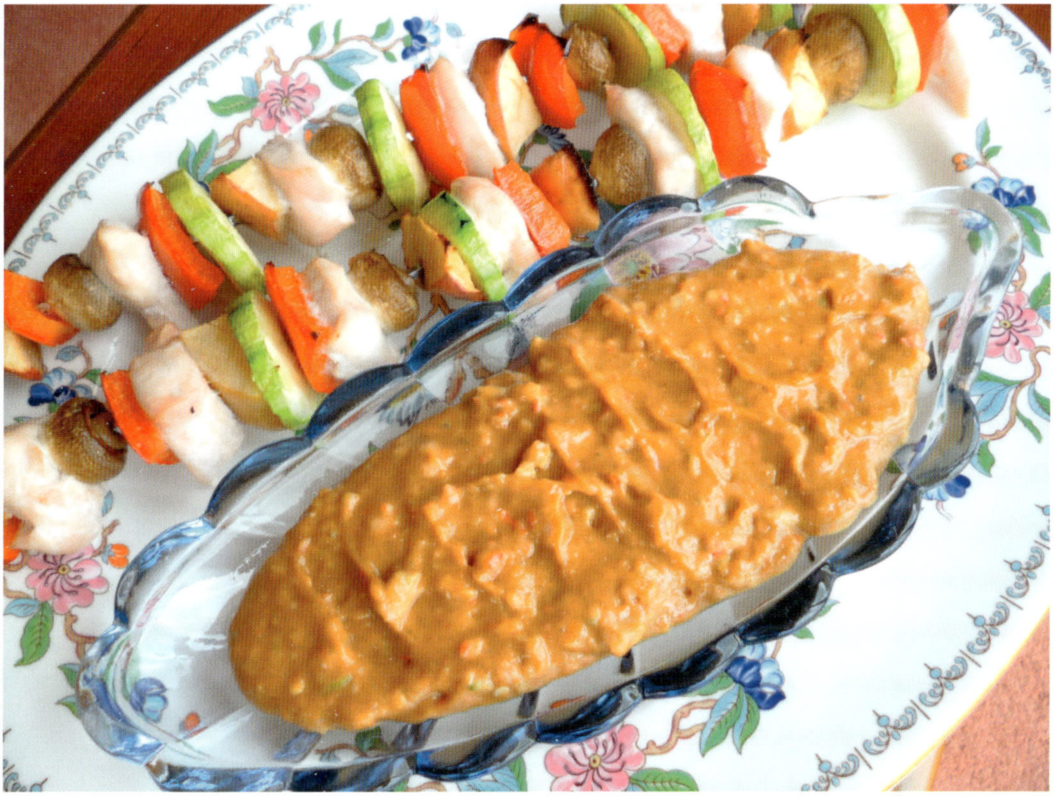

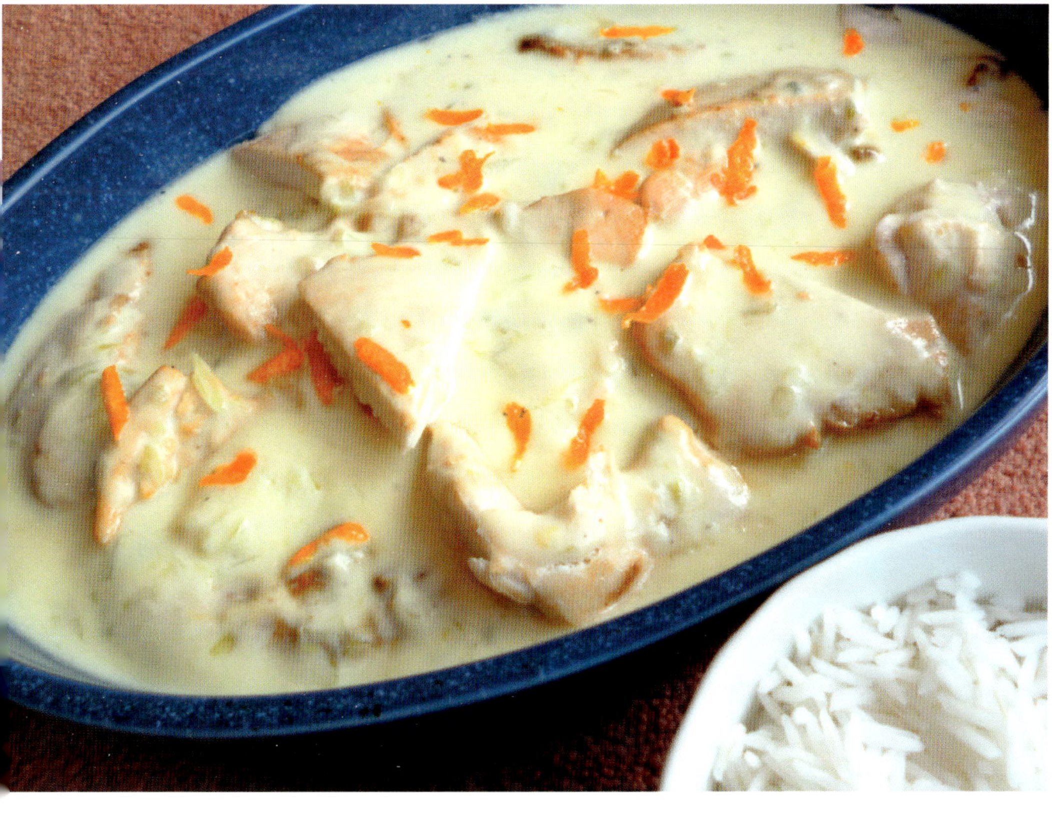

## Barbecue Chicken Marinade

**Ingredients:**

| | |
|---|---|
| 2 lemon grass stalks, chopped | 15mil/1 tablespoon soft brown sugar |
| 2.5cm/1in piece fresh root ginger | 120ml/4fl oz coconut milk |
| 6 garlic gloves | 30ml/2 tablespoons fish sauce |
| 4 shallots | 30ml/2 tablespoons soy sauce |
| Half bunch coriander | 8 to 12 small pieces chicken |

Method:

Place all the ingredients (but not the chicken pieces) into a food processor and process until smooth, then put the small pieces of chicken in a dish and pour over the marinade.

Leave in a cool place overnight to let the flavour develop.

Pre-heat the oven to 200°C / 400°F / Gas mark 6.

Put the chicken pieces on a baking tray and brush more marinade on top of them and bake in the oven for 20 to 30 minutes.

Turn the chicken half-way through cooking and brush with more marinade.

Serve with boiled rice.

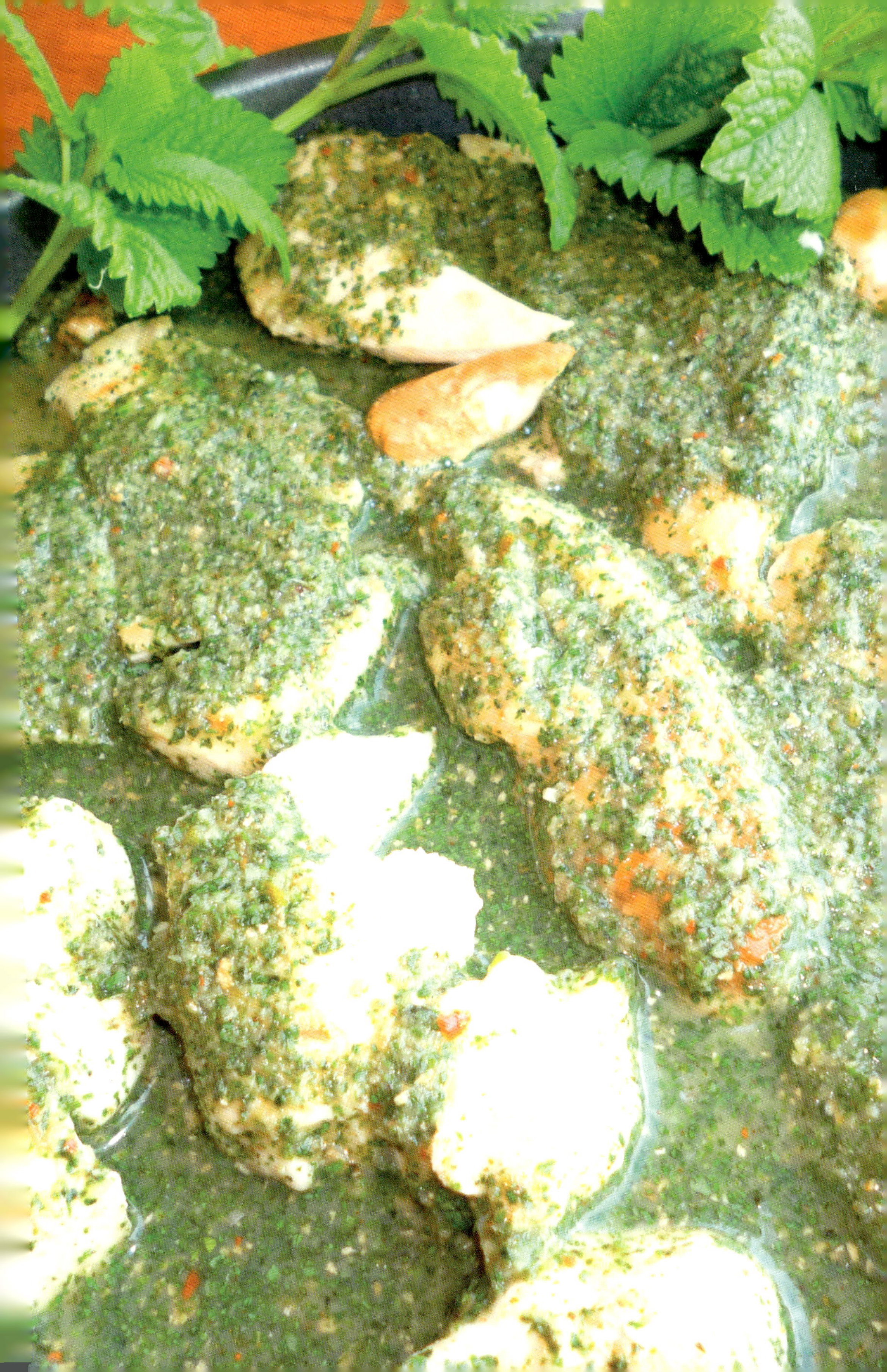

## Garlic and Chilli Cream
for cold chicken pieces

**Ingredients:**

**2 thick slices farmhouse or natural white bread (cut off the crusts)**
**Water for soaking**
**2 cloves garlic, crushed**
**1 red chilli, finely chopped, remove seeds**
**1 egg yolk**
**Salt and black pepper to taste**
**2 tablespoons olive oil.**

**Method:**

Place bread and enough water to soak for 5 minutes.

Squeeze water from the bread and put the bread in the food processor with garlic, chilli, yolk, salt and pepper.

Process for 20 seconds. With motor still going, add oil in a slow steady stream.

Transfer to a serving bowl, cover and chill in the fridge.


## Cherry Sauce
for pheasant or duck

**Ingredients:**

**1 orange (juice and zest)**
**1 teaspoon ground ginger**
**1 lemon (juice)**
**1 tablespoon soy sauce**
**60ml port**
**410g cherries, pitted and reserve the juice**
**1 tablespoon cornflour**

**Method:**

Put all the ingredients into a saucepan over a moderate heat, bring to the boil then reduce and cook for 5 minutes.

Meanwhile mix the cold reserved cherry juice with the cornflour. Stir this into the pan until the sauce thickens.

Use this sauce with cooked pheasant or duck.

Note: Leave pheasant or duck in red wine overnight before cooking as this will make the meat deliciously tender.

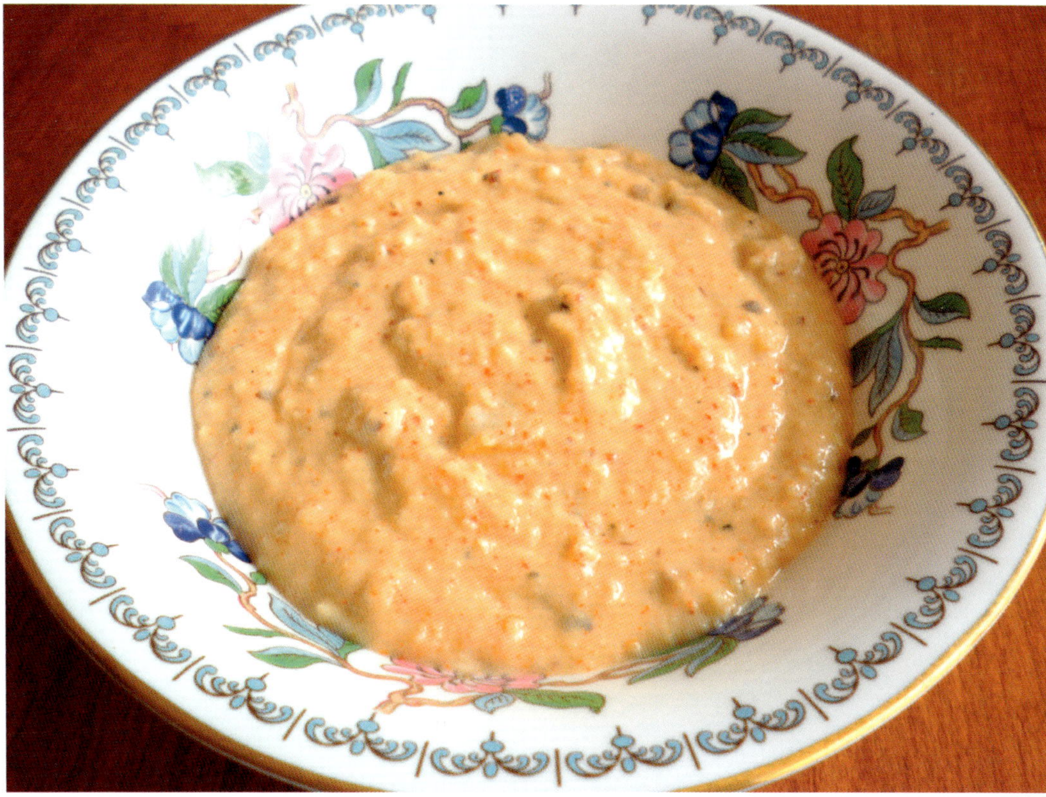

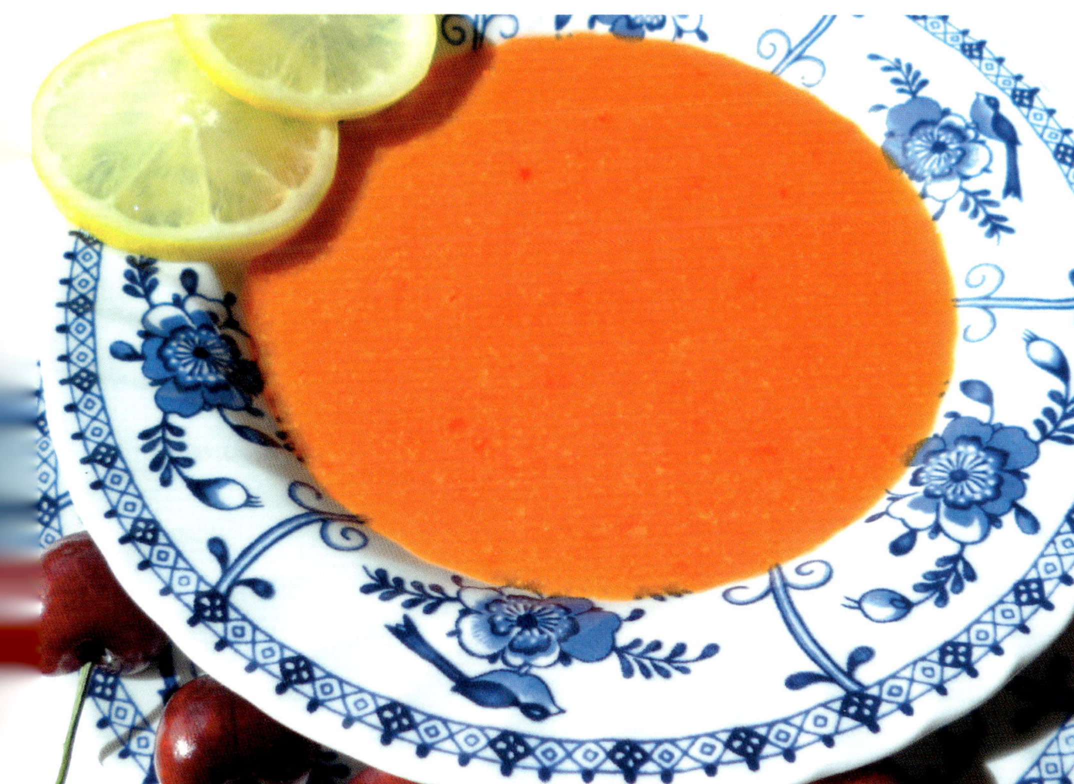

## Mixed Fruit Sauce
for guinea foul

**Ingredients:**

**240ml water**
**700g apples, plums and pears, chopped**
**180ml apple juice**
**1 tablespoon apricot jam**
**100g soft brown sugar**
**2 cloves garlic (crushed)**
**Pinch of dry English mustard**

**Method:**

Place all the ingredients into a saucepan over a medium heat and bring to the boil, stirring frequently until the fruit has softened.

Remove from the heat, let cool then blend in the blender or food processor until smooth.

Cover and place in the fridge until needed.

## Sweet Orange Marinade
for pheasant, duck or guinea foul

**Ingredients:**

**1 orange, chopped**
**Half teaspoon of ground ginger**
**3 cups red wine**
**1 tablespoon Raspberry jam**
**1 teaspoon English mustard**
**1 lime (juiced)**
**2 teaspoons soy sauce**
**Small pinch salt**

**Method:**

Place all the ingredients into a shallow dish and mix well.

Add the pheasant, duck or guinea foul to the marinade and leave overnight ready to put into a slow oven the next day to cook slowly for 4 hours.

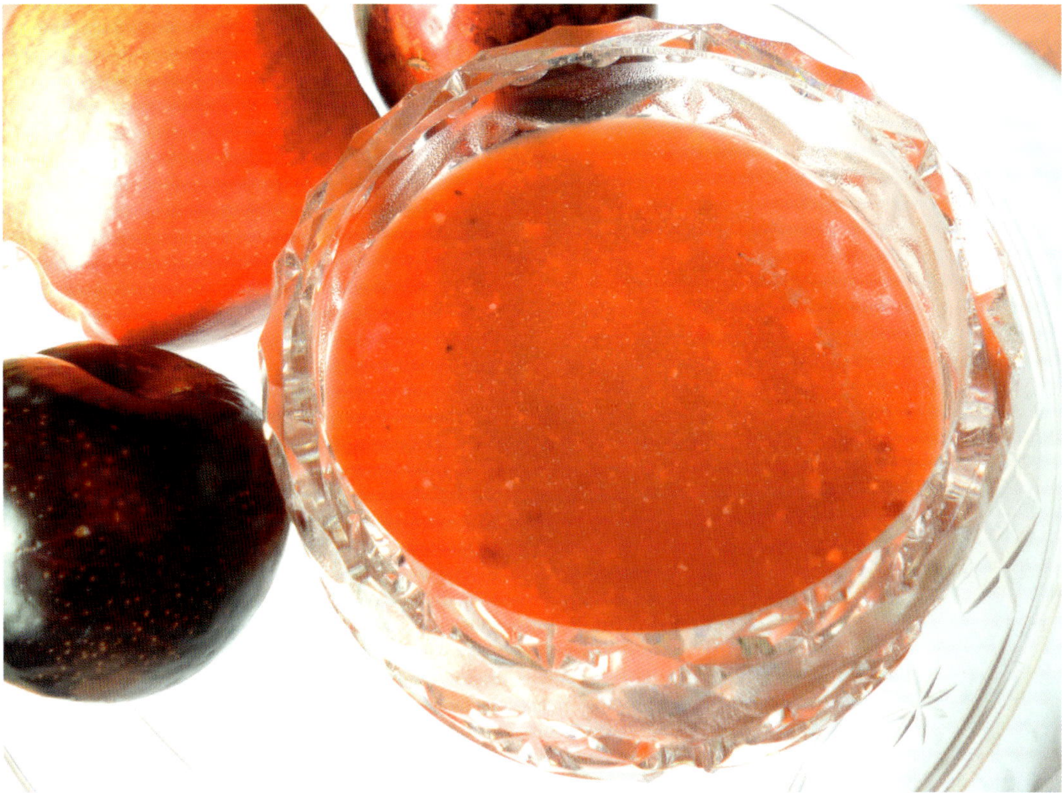

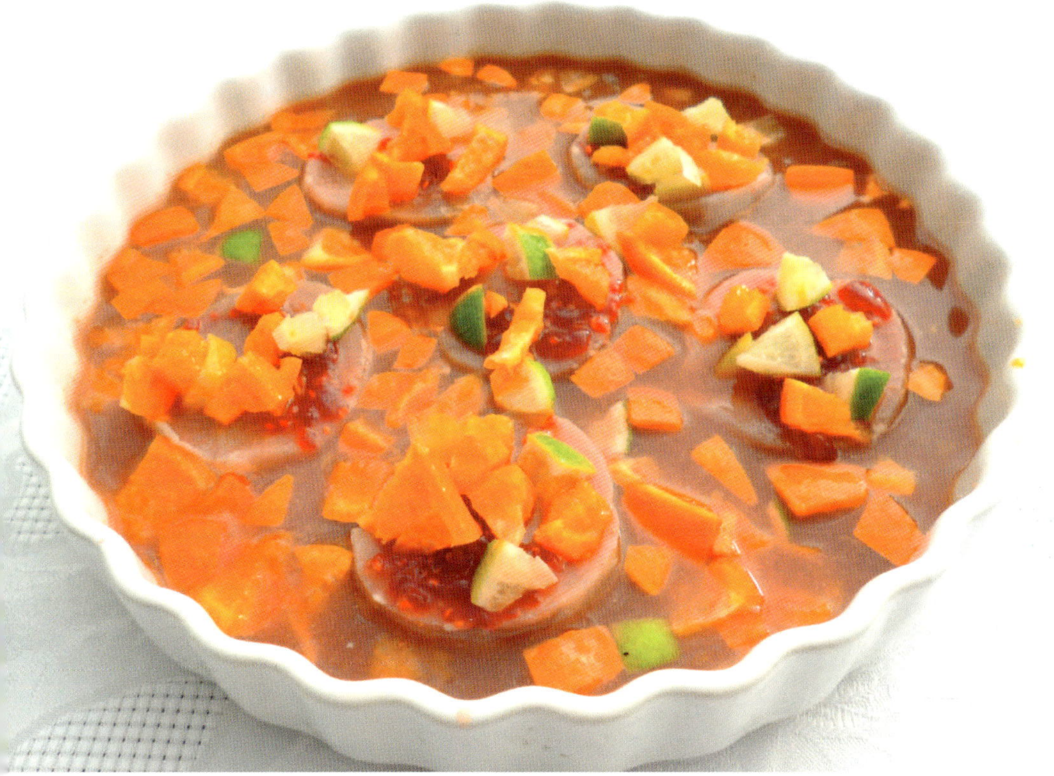

## Red Wine Sauce
for duck

**Ingredients:**

**120ml dry red wine**
**40ml olive oil**
**40ml light soy sauce**
**1 tablespoon orange juice**
**1 tablespoon cranberry jelly**
**1 heaped teaspoon cornflour**
**Salt and pepper to taste**

Method:

Place all the ingredients into a sauce pan and mix well, making sure the cornflour is thoroughly mixed.

Turn up the heat and bring to the boil then turn down the heat and stir continuously until the sauce has come together and thickened.

Remove from heat and let cool ready to serve.

## Mixed spice and yoghurt Sauce
tasty and different for chicken

**Ingredients:**

**1 large onion**
**25g/1oz butter**
**1 tablespoon plain flour**
**6fl oz/175ml chicken stock**
**Pinch of salt and pepper**
**Large pinch of mixed spice**
**4 tablespoons natural yoghurt**

Method:

Peel, dice and chop the onion into small pieces, melt the butter in a sauce pan and fry the onion until soft.

Stir in the flour and gradually add the stock, allowing the mixture to thicken, add the seasoning.

When mixture has thickened remove from heat and allow to cool, then add the yoghurt, mix together and serve.

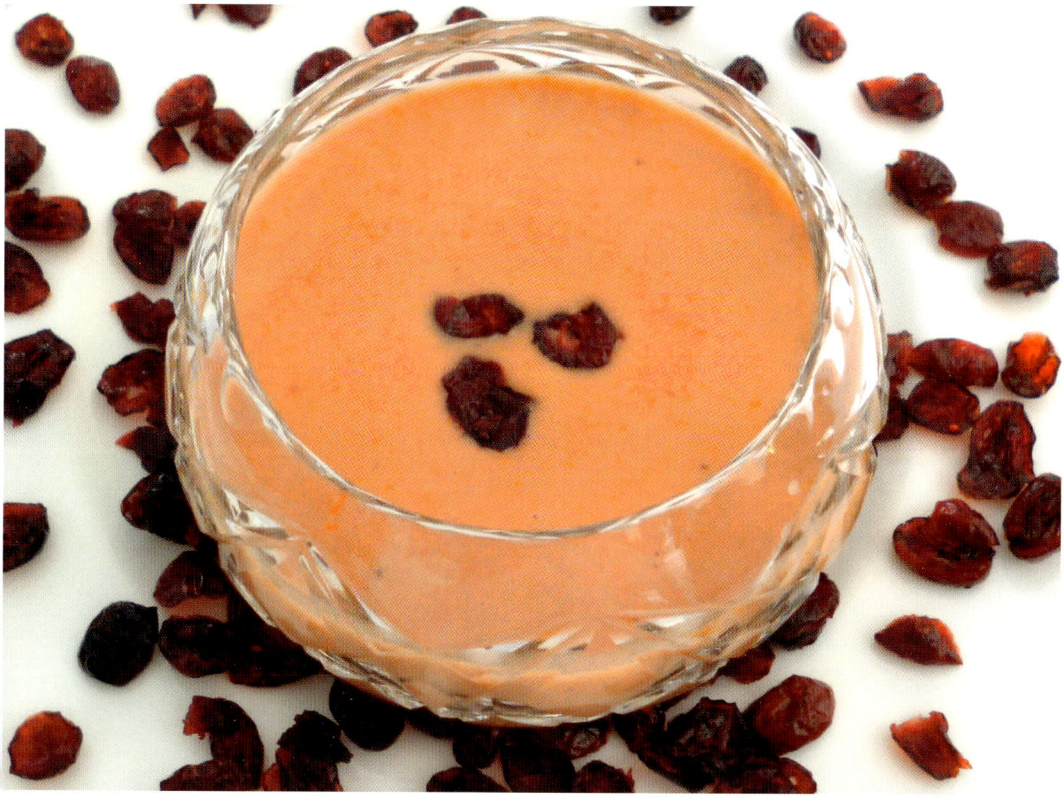

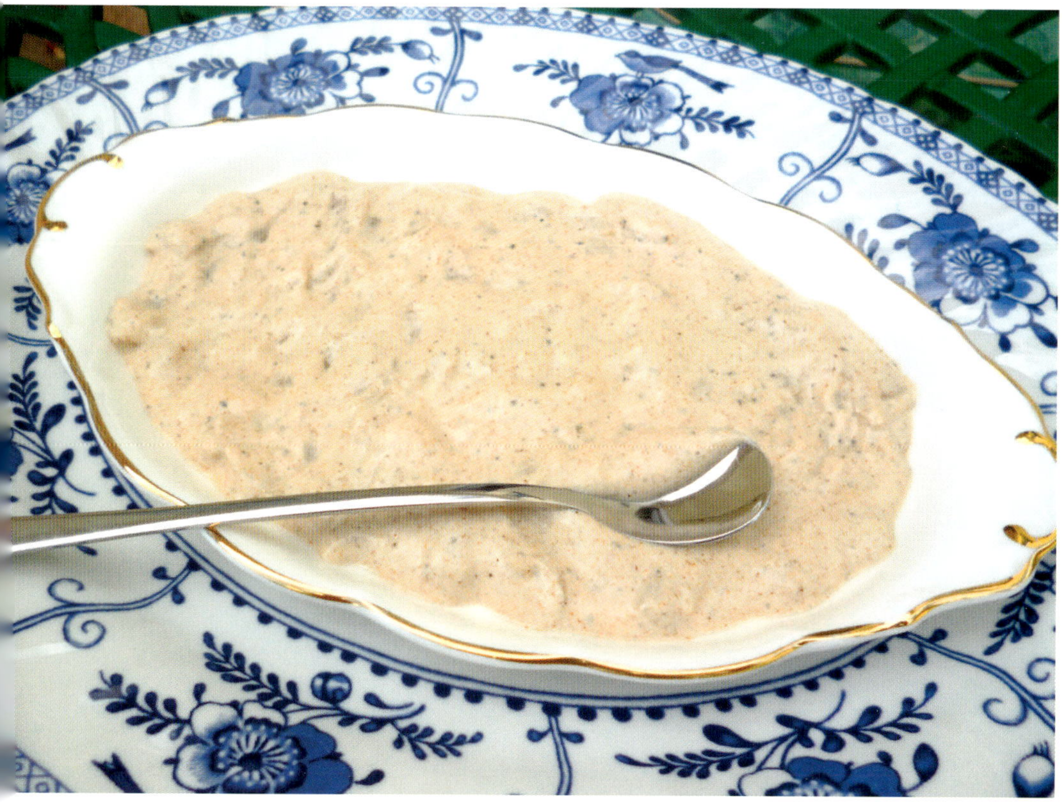

## Red Wine Marinade
for pheasant

**Ingredients:**

**Whole oven ready pheasant**
**1oz butter**
**2 tablespoons olive oil**
**2 bacon rashers, chopped**
**250 red wine**

**250 chicken stock**
**1 tablespoon Worcester sauce and 2 tablespoons bramble jelly**
**1 teaspoon each of rosemary and thyme**
**3 bay leaves (remove after cooking)**

Method:

Place the whole prepared bird in the frying pan with butter and olive oil, turn and seal for 10 minutes.

Put pheasant into a saucepan together with the fried chopped bacon, the wine, chicken stock, Worcester sauce, bramble jelly and herbs.

Bring to the boil and cook for 10 minutes.

Transfer everything from the pan into a casserole dish and place in a low oven 200°F and cook for 3 to 4 hours.

Remove from the oven and let cool and remove all bones.

Cook for a further 15 mins in the oven.

Serve with new potatoes and green vegetables. Delicious.

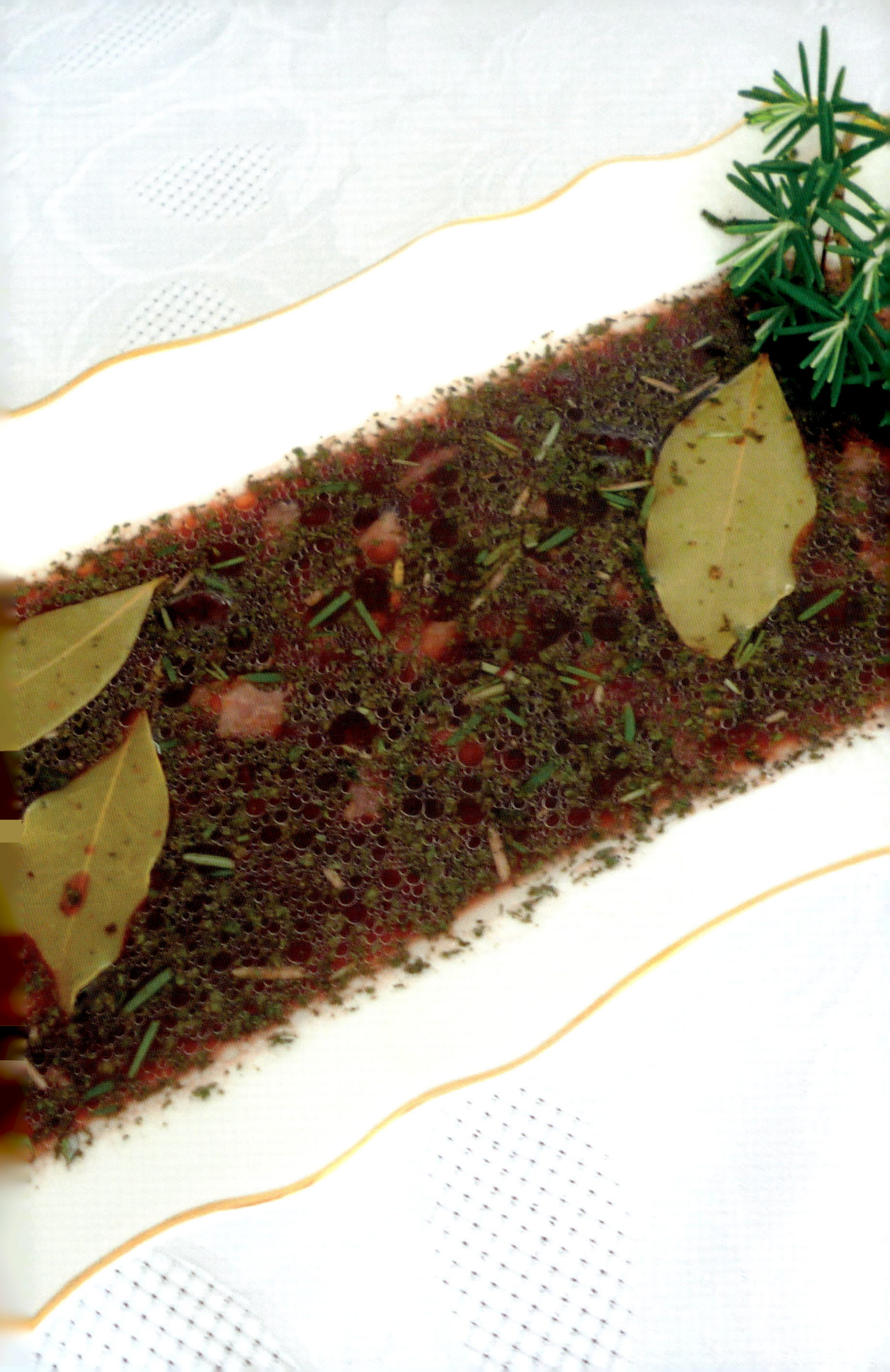

~ Desserts ~

## Creamy Chocolate Sauce

**Ingredients:**

**10fl oz/275ml milk**
**1 tablespoon cocoa**
**1g plain chocolate**
**1 dessertspoon corn flour**
**1 dessertspoon sugar**

**Method:**

Melt chocolate in a bowl sitting in another bowl of hot water.

Put all the ingredients into an electric blender for a few seconds.

Pour into a saucepan and heat slowly, stirring all the time for 2 or 3 minutes.

## Amaretto Sauce

**Ingredients:**

**3 tablespoons cornflour**
**400ml/14fl oz whole milk**
**40g caster sugar**
**1 teaspoon vanilla extract**
**2 tablespoons amaretto liqueur**
**100ml double cream**

**Method:**

Place the cornflour in a bowl with 3 tablespoons of the milk and mix.

Pour the remaining milk into a pan and add the caster sugar and the cornflour mixture.

Bring to the boil, whisking constantly until the sauce thickens. Take off the heat and stir in the vanilla extract, amaretto and the cream.

Serve warm or leave to cool to room temperature. Put some greaseproof paper on the surface to stop a skin forming.

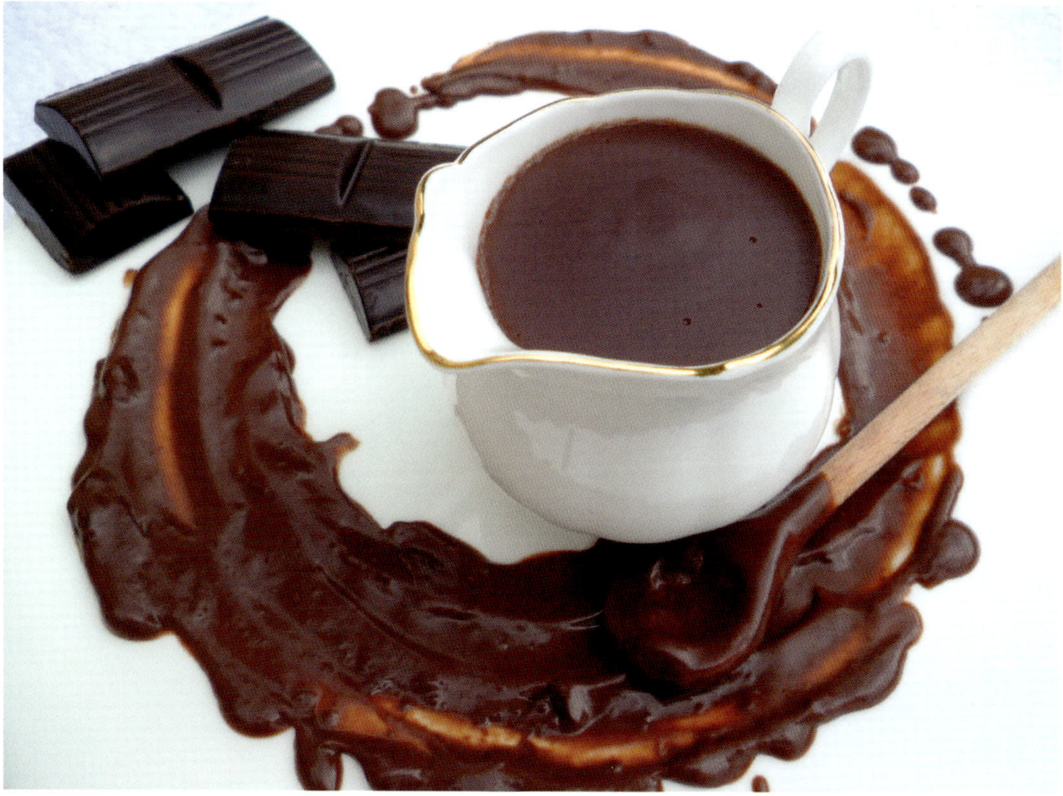

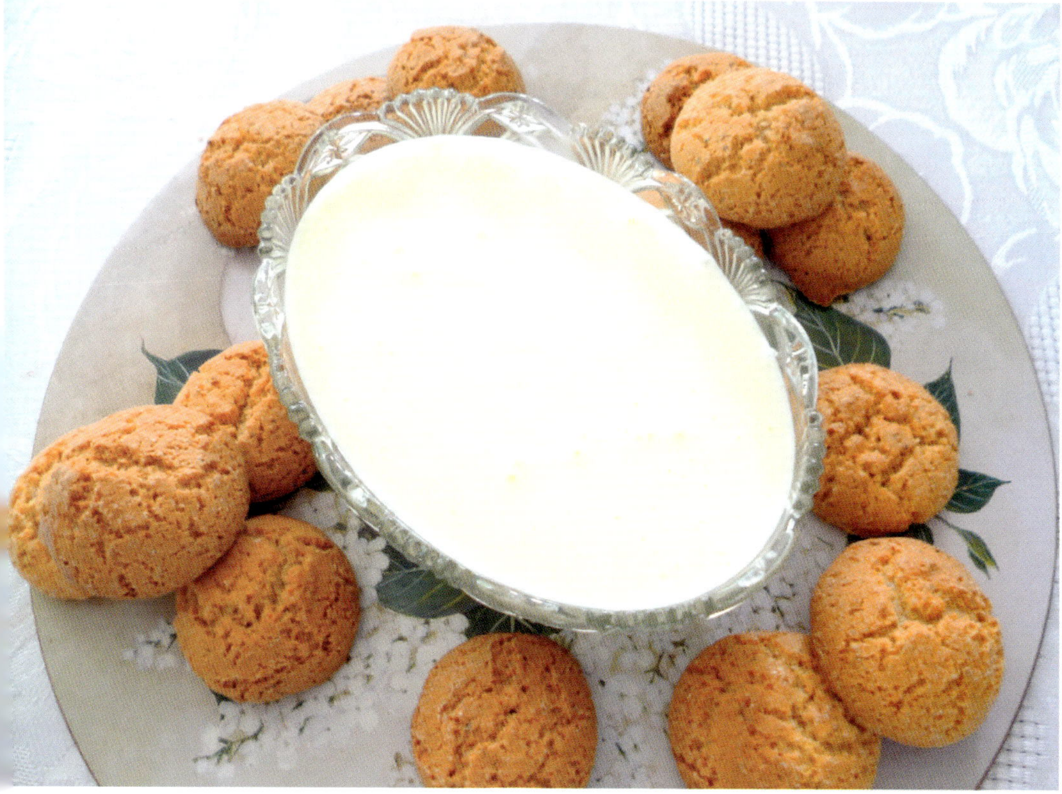

## Lemon Sauce

**Ingredients:**

**10fl oz/275ml water**
**1g cornflour**
**2 tablespoons sugar**
**Juice of 1 lemon**
**A little butter**
**1 teaspoon lemon curd**

Method:

Blend all the ingredients together and put into a saucepan and cook for 2 to 3 minutes, stirring all the time until creamy.

## Brandy Sauce
for Christmas pudding or mince pies

**Ingredients:**

**75g plain flour**
**75g butter**
**75g caster sugar**
**16fl oz/450ml milk**
**4 tablespoons brandy**

Method:

Melt the butter in a saucepan slowly and stir the flour into the melted butter until smooth.

Add the milk slowly and stir well avoiding any lumps. Stir in the sugar and cook on a very low heat for 10 to 12 minutes.

Keep stirring slowly as the mixture may stick.

Add the brandy. Now ready to serve.

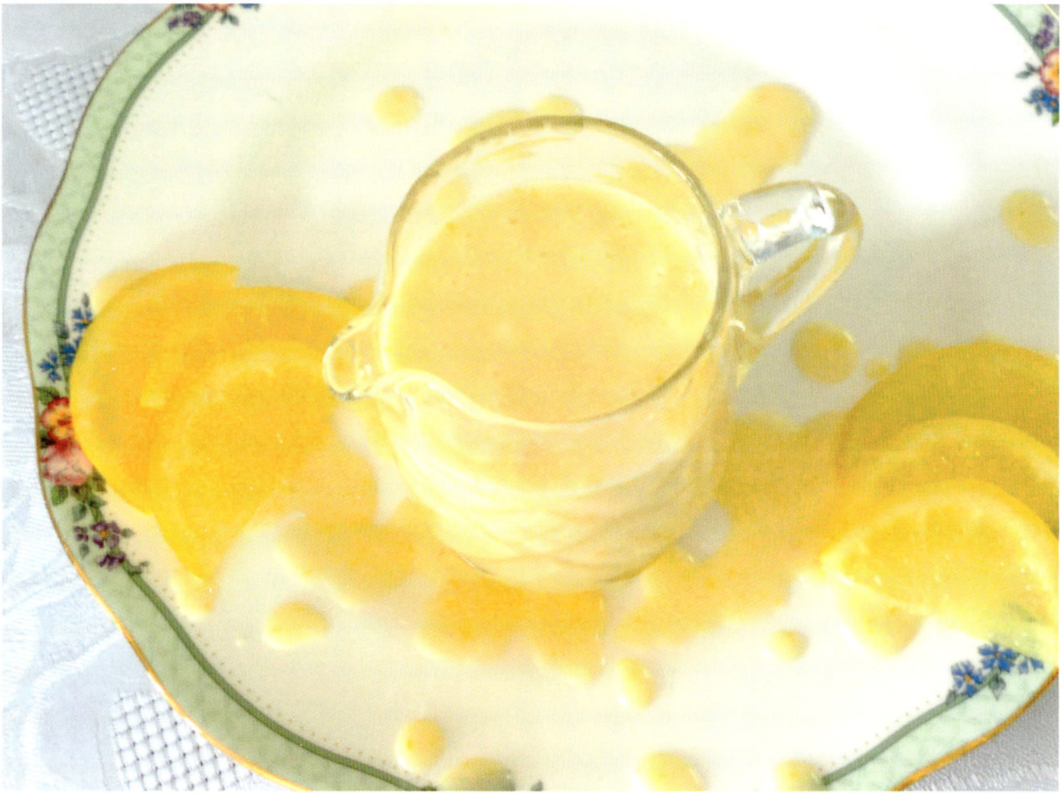

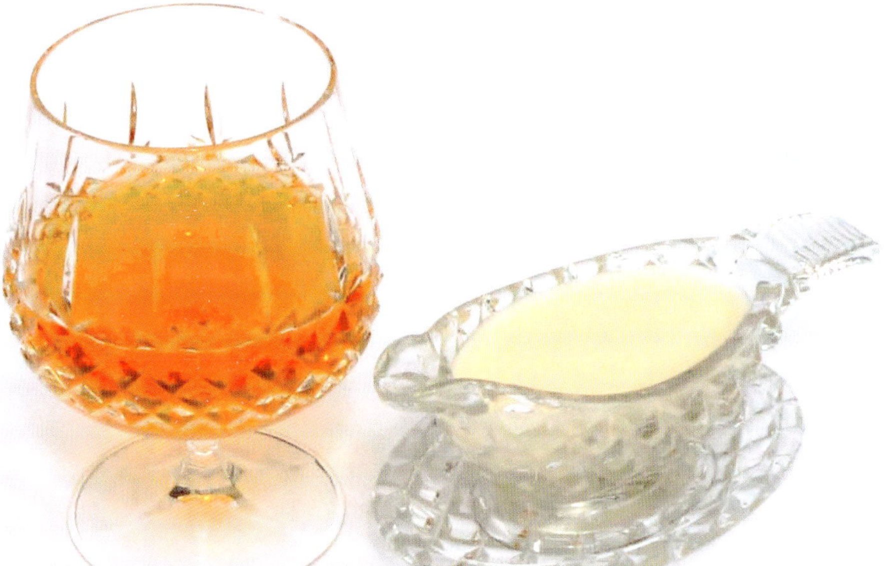

## Butterscotch Sauce
for ice cream

**Ingredients:**

**75g soft brown sugar**
**150g golden syrup**
**4fl oz/110ml double cream**
**50g butter or margarine**
**40g caster sugar**
**A little vanilla essence**

Method:

Put the soft brown sugar, syrup, butter/margarine and caster sugar into a pan.

Slowly heat and once the sugar has dissolved and everything is liquid continue to heat for 6 minutes stirring all the time.

Remove from the heat and slowly stir in the double cream and a little vanilla essence. Stir until the mixture is smooth.

This can be served hot or cold and can be stored in a cool place for another few days.

## Raspberry and Honey Sauce
for sponges, jellies or ice-cream

**Ingredients:**

**One handful of fresh raspberries**
**1 tablespoonful of honey**
**1 small tub of natural yoghurt**

Method:

Blend the raspberries and honey together and if you want to discard the seeds, push the mixture through a fine sieve then add the yoghurt and mix together thoroughly.

Very quick, healthy and very tasty.

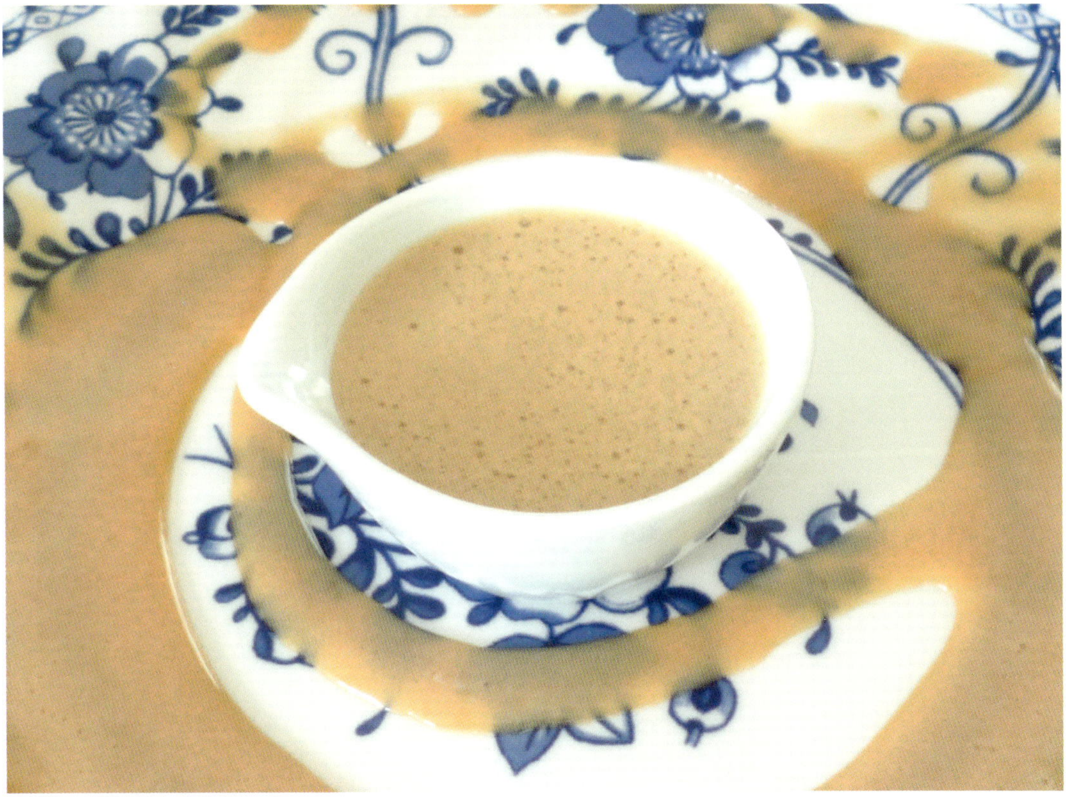

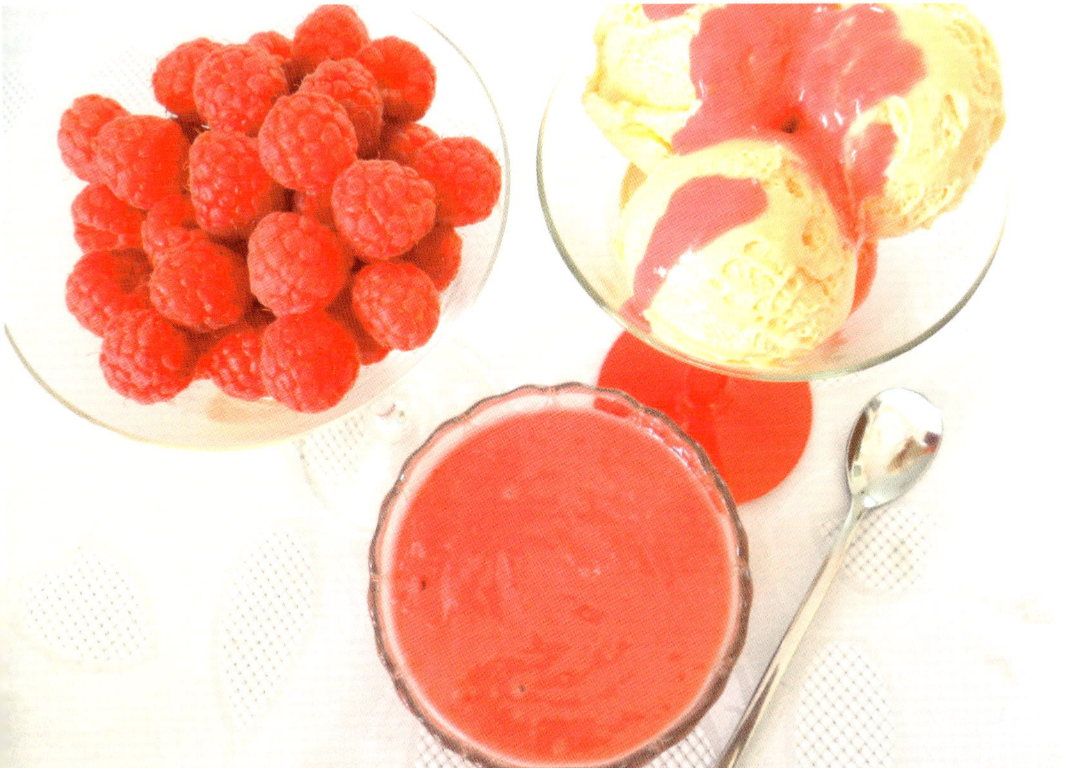

## Strawberry Sauce

**Ingredients:**

**250g strawberries**
**100g soft light brown sugar**
**1 tablespoon lemon juice**

Method:

Pureé the strawberries with the lemon juice, then pass the strawberry pureé through a sieve to remove the tiny pips. Put the sugar in a pan with 2 tablespoons of water and dissolve over a low heat. Bring to the boil, then stir until the caramel mixture blends together.

Remove from heat and add the strawberry pureé with the lemon juice. Stir until all the caramel is incorporated then leave to cool.

This sauce goes well with slices of pineapple and ice-cream.

## Chocolate Sauce
for fruit or sponges

**Ingredients:**

**100ml single cream**
**100g plain chocolate**
**2 tablespoons Grand Marnier**

Method:

Break the chocolate into squares and place in a heat-proof bowl and put the bowl over a saucepan of hot water and melt the chocolate, careful not to burn it as it doesn't take long.

When melted remove from the heat and add the single cream and Grand Marnier and blend with an electric whisk.

This sauce is very nice as a base with blanched apple slices or tinned pears on top in small bowls.

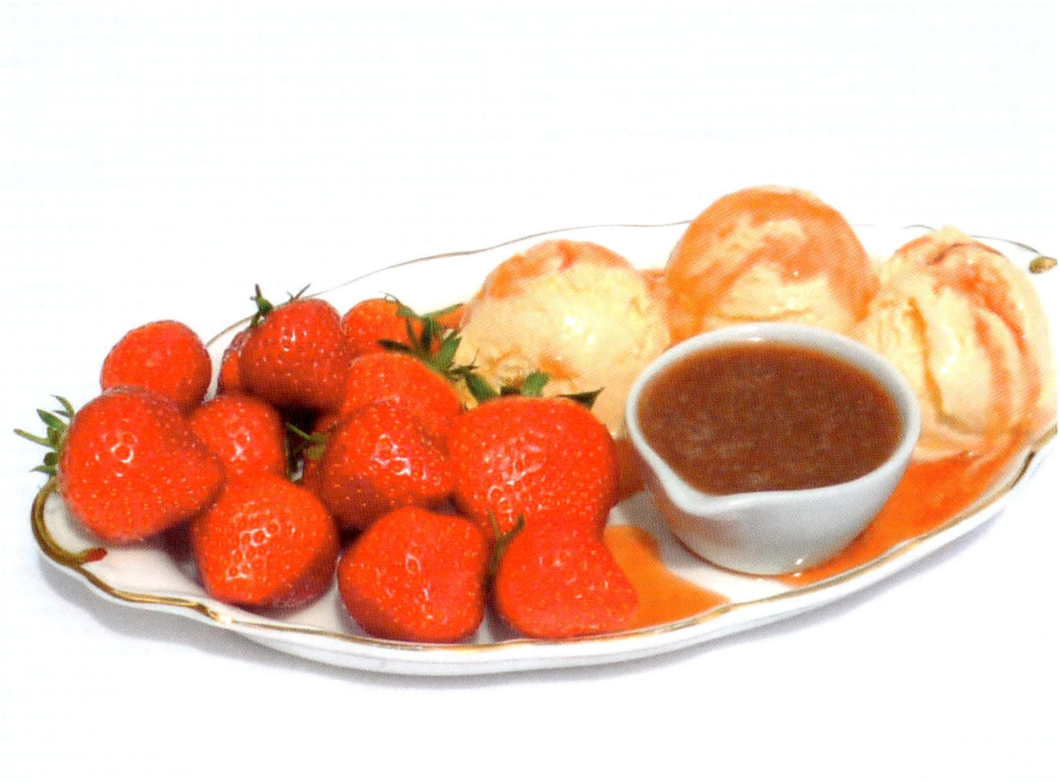

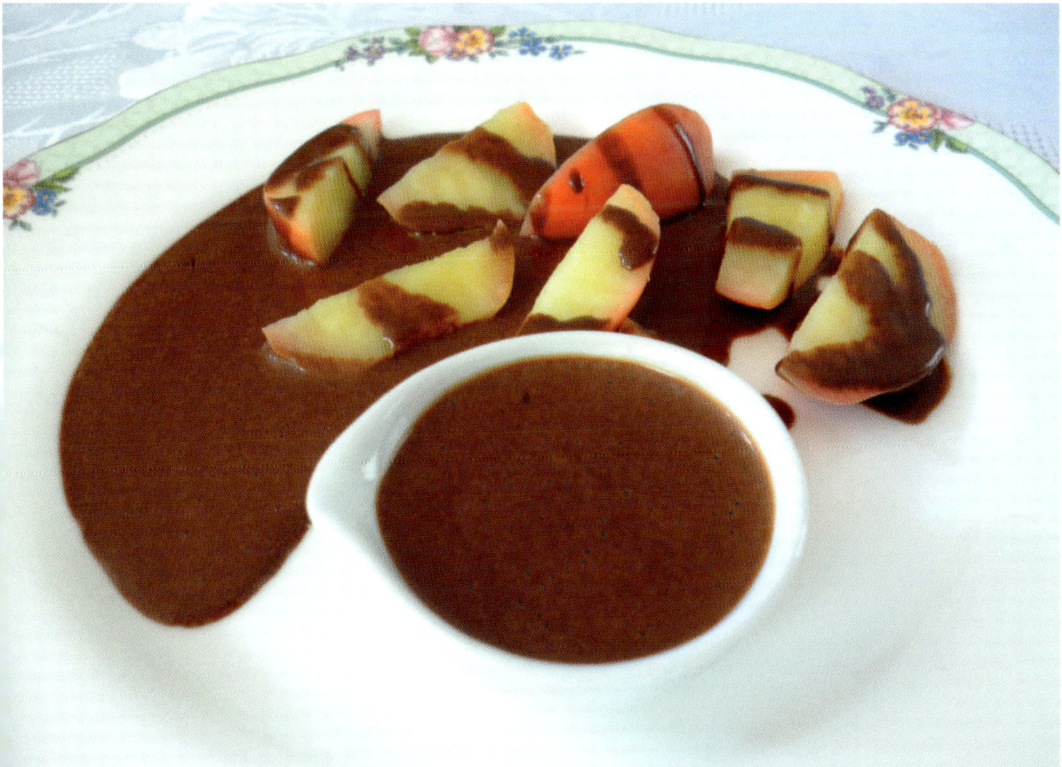

## Fresh Vanilla Custard Sauce
for sponge or fruit pies

**Ingredients:**

**300ml full-fat milk**
**Half tablespoon vanilla extract**
**3 large egg yokes**
**2 tablespoons golden caster sugar**
**1 tablespoon cornflour**

**Method:**

Pour the milk into a saucepan and bring to the boil, add the vanilla extract. Turn off the heat and leave to cool for 5 minutes. Put the egg yolks, sugar and cornflour in a bowl and whisk together then gradually whisk in the milk.

Return to the heat, whisking continuously for 2 - 3 minutes or until the mixture thickens. It should just coat the back of a wooden spoon.

Serve immediately with vanilla sponge or fruit pies and tarts.

## Grand Marnier Cream

**Ingredients:**

**284ml carton double cream**
**1 tablespoon golden caster sugar**
**2 tablespoons Grand Marnier**
**Grated zest of 1 orange**

**Method:**

Whip the cream with the sugar until soft peaks are formed.

Stir in the Grand Marnier and half the gated orange zest then spoon onto a serving dish.

Cover and chill until needed.

Finally when serving put the remaining orange zest onto the cream on the dessert.

This goes well with chocolate brownies.

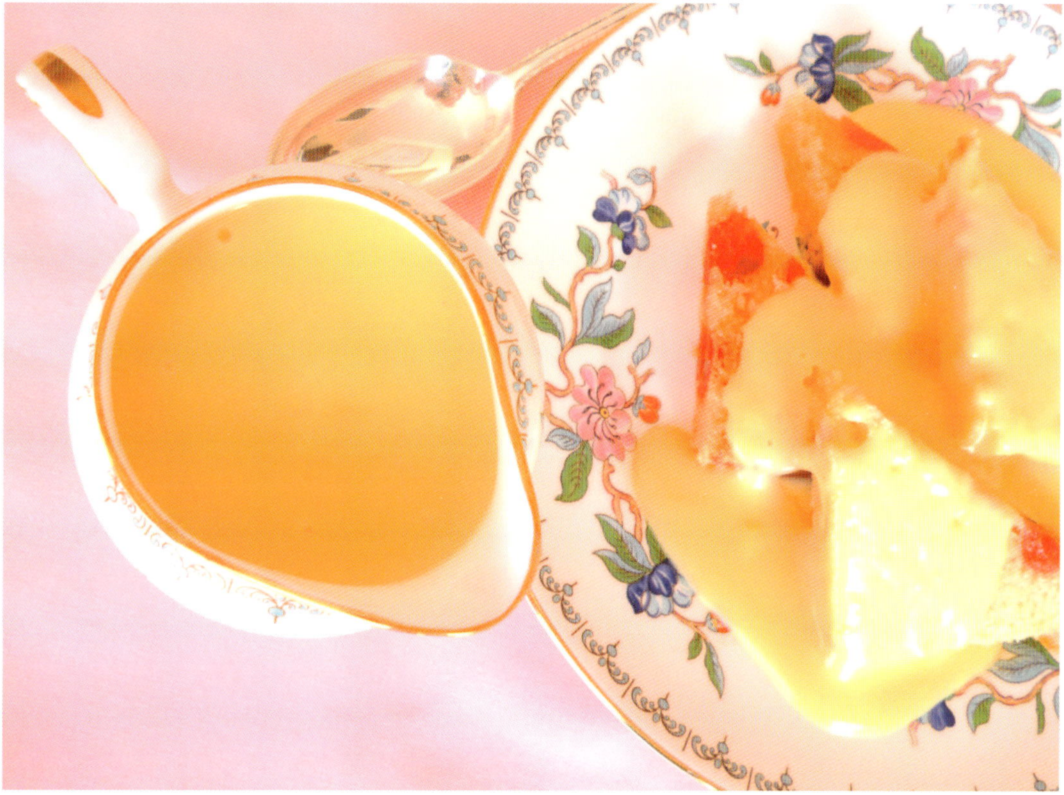

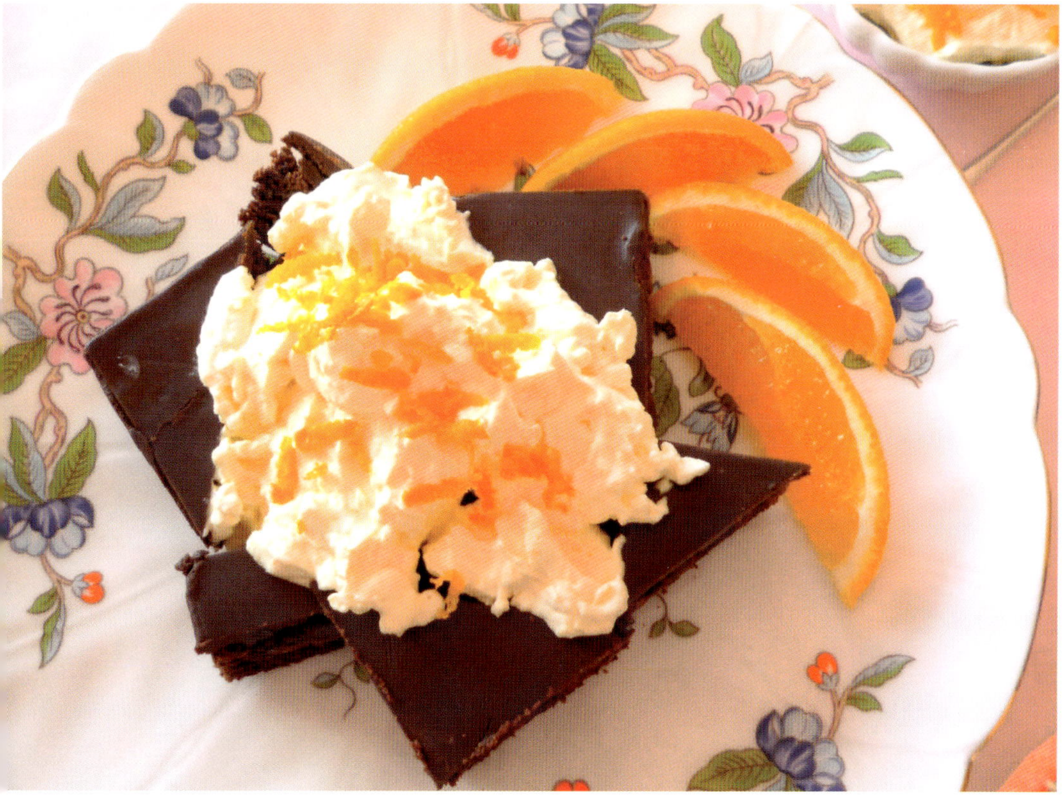

## Whipped Brandy Butter
for Christmas Pudding or Mince Pies

**Ingredients:**

**150g/5oz unsalted butter (at room temperature)**
**150g/5oz golden icing sugar**
**3 tablespoons brandy**

**Method:**

Place the butter in a bowl and whisk and gradually add the icing sugar, whisking all the time until it's almost used up then pour in the brandy.

Continue whisking until the mixture is pale and fluffy.

Spoon into a serving dish.

Cover and chill until needed.

Remove from the fridge 3 minutes before serving.


## Granola topping
for natural yoghurt or on stewed fruit

**Ingredients:**

**120ml/4fl oz sunflower oil**
**90ml/3fl oz malt extract**
**90ml/3fl oz clear honey**
**250g/8oz rolled oats**
**250g/8oz large oat flakes**
**125g/4oz hazelnuts**
**25g/1oz desiccated coconut**
**50g/2oz sunflower seeds**
**25g/1oz sesame seeds**

**Method:**

Place oil, malt and honey in a large pan and heat gently until the malt is runny. Mix in the remaining ingredients and stir thoroughly.

Turn into a large roasting tin and bake in a preheated moderately hot oven, 190°C / 375°F / Gas mark 5, for 30 to 35 minutes, stirring occasionally.

Leave to cool then separate the pieces with your fingers.

Store in an airtight container.

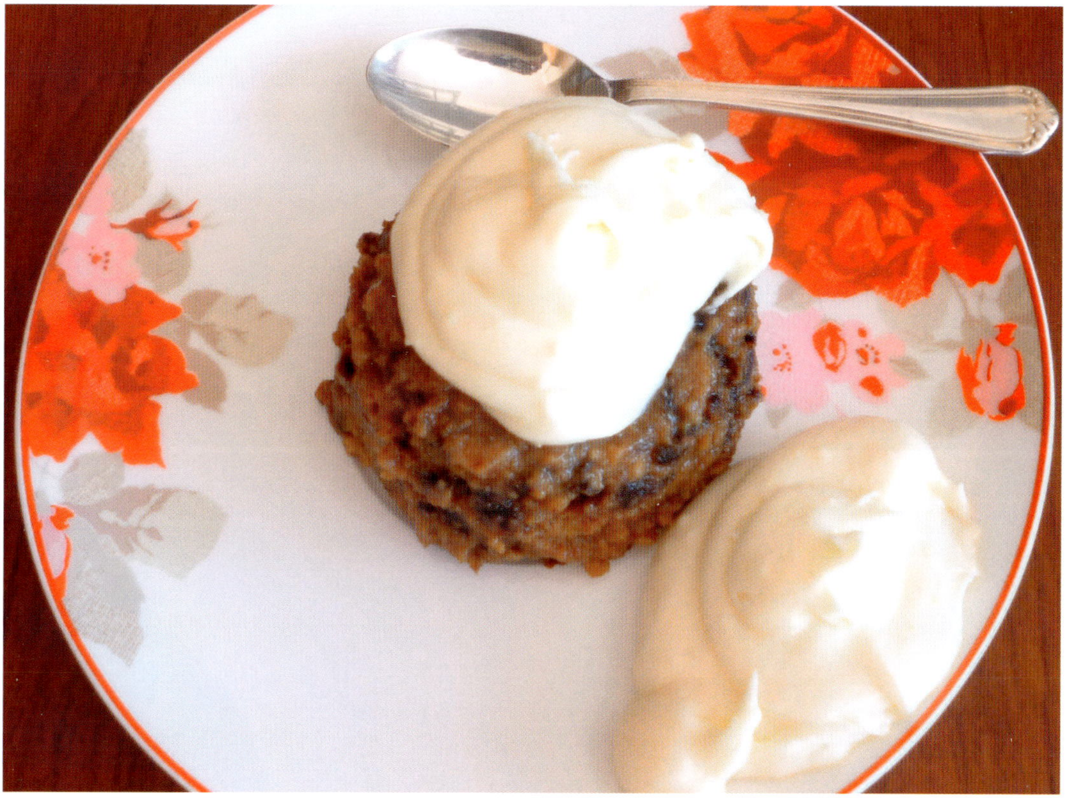

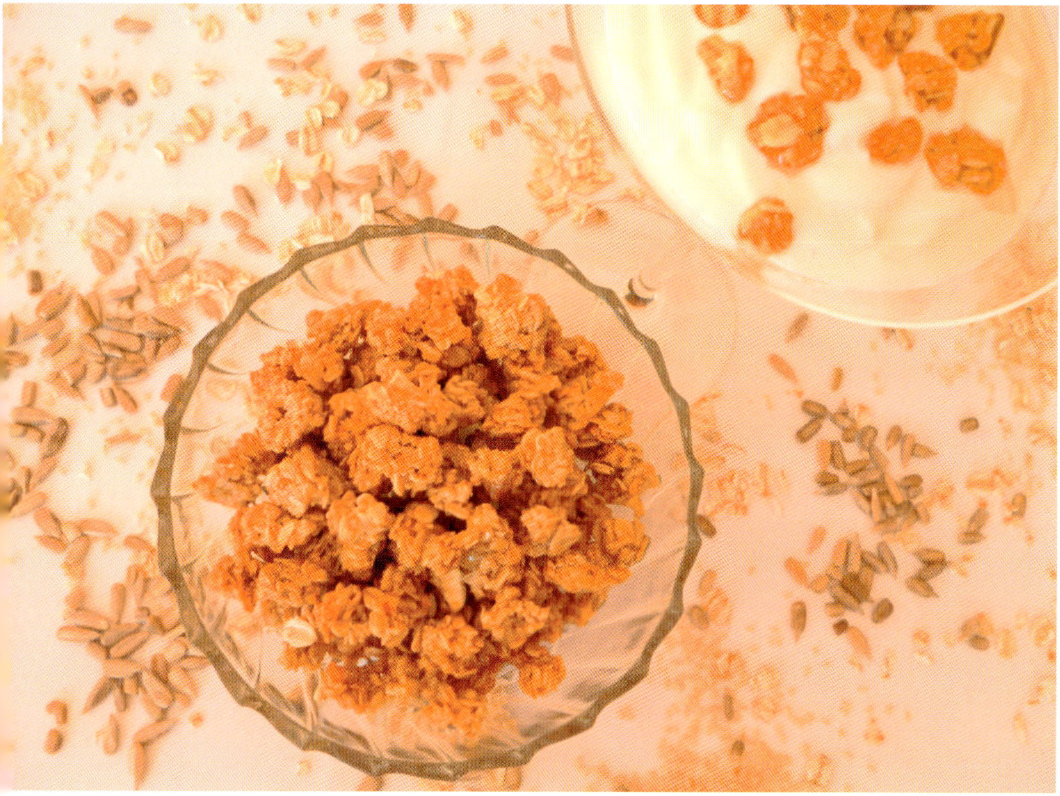

## Highland Cream Sauce
for fresh fruit salad

**Ingredients:**

**25g/1oz blanched almonds, chopped**
**25g/1oz medium oatmeal**
**25g/1oz whole wheat breadcrumbs**
**142ml/5floz double cream**
**3 tablespoons whisky**
**2 tablespoons runny honey**
**150g/5oz natural yoghurt**

**Method:**

Mix the almonds, oatmeal and breadcrumbs together and place on a baking sheet or tray under a pre-heated grill until golden brown, stirring from time to time, then remove and leave to cool.

In a clean bowl mix the double cream, whisky and honey together until soft peaks form then fold in the yoghurt and the cooled almond mixture.

Chill until ready to serve with fresh fruit salad or hot apple pie.

## Yoghurt Snow Cream

**Ingredients:**

**2 egg whites**
**3 tablespoons runny honey**
**300g/10oz natural yoghurt**

**Method:**

Whisk the egg whites until stiff then add the honey and whisk until very thick.

Fold in the yoghurt and serve immediately.

This is an ideal alternative to double cream.

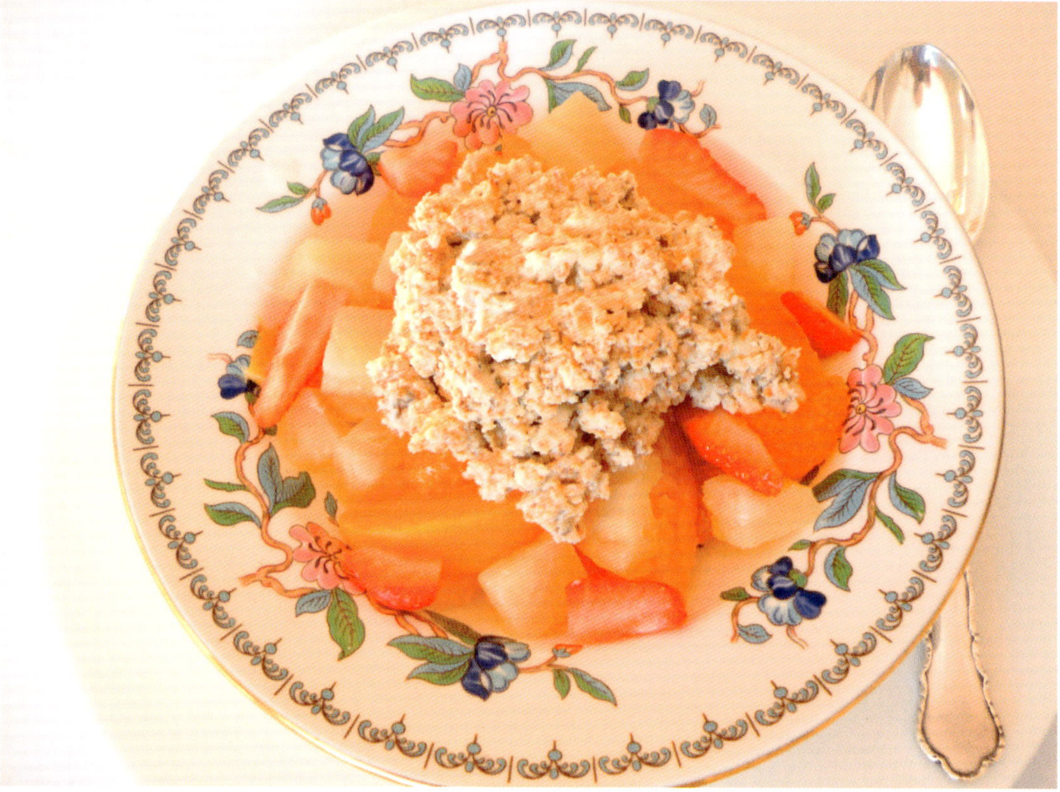

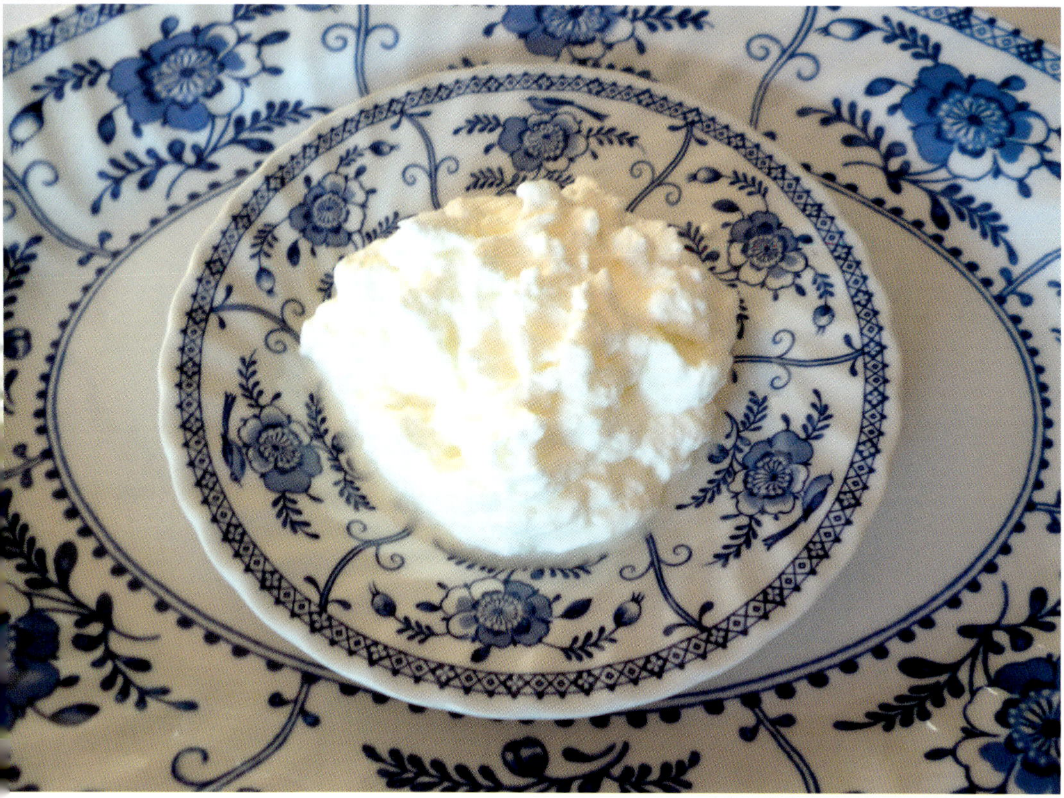

# Banana Ice Cream

**Ingredients:**

**6 ripe bananas chopped**
**5 tablespoons milk**
**2 tablespoons runny honey**
**15g flaked toasted almonds**

**Method:**

Cut the bananas into slices and put the pieces into a food processor, add the milk and honey and whisk/blitz until creamy. Place in the freezer in a plastic container for 1 to 2 hours, check the cream after 1 hour as you want the mixture cold and firm but not frozen, then spoon the cream into bowls and serve immediately, topped with a sprinkle of flaked toasted almonds.

Note: You can keep the banana cream in the freezer for up to one month but remember to let the cream rest in room temperature to soften a little so that you can spoon it out.

# Apricot Whipped Mousse

**Ingredients:**

**400g/14oz tin of apricots**
**15ml/1 tablespoon Grand Marnier or Brandy**
**175g/6oz low flat natural yoghurt**
**30ml/2 teaspoons flaked almonds**

**Method:**

Drain the juice from the apricots and place the fruit together with the liqueur in a blender or food processor, process until smooth. Put an alternate spoonful of the fruit purée then a spoonful of the yoghurt into four tall glasses or dishes. Finally, swirling the two mixtures together slightly to make a marbled effect. Lightly toast the almonds until they are golden brown. Let them cool then sprinkle some on top of the mousse.

If you don't want to use the liqueur then put a little of the fruit juice from the apricots instead.

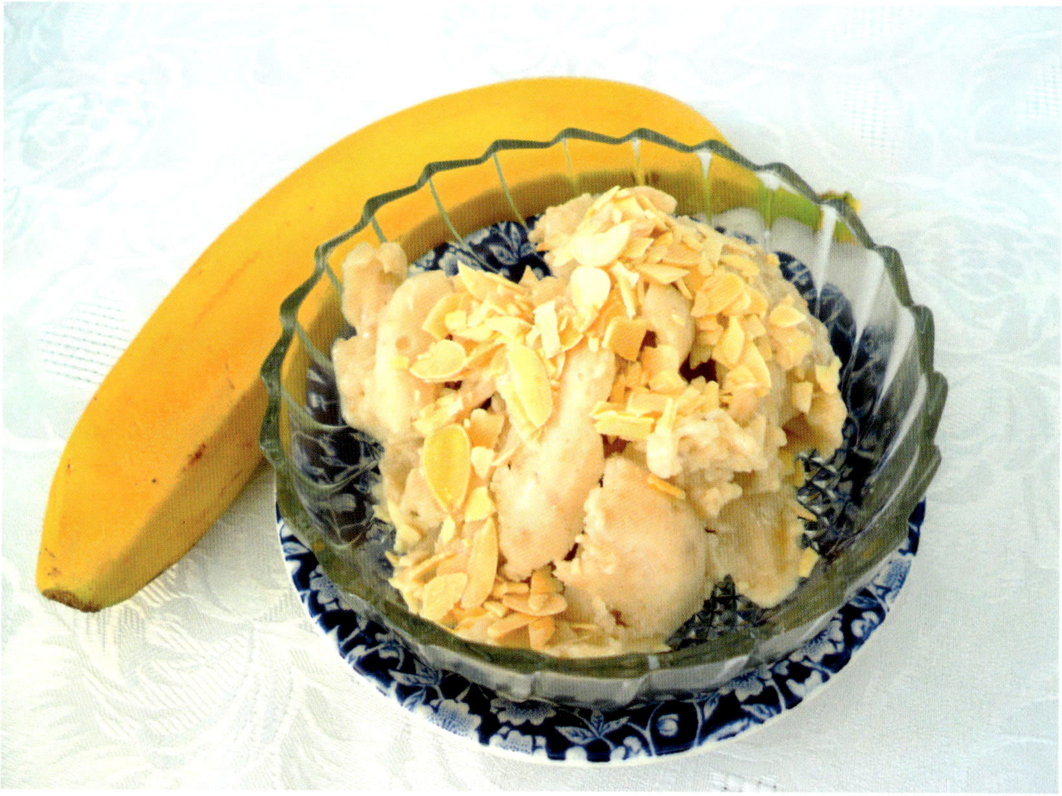

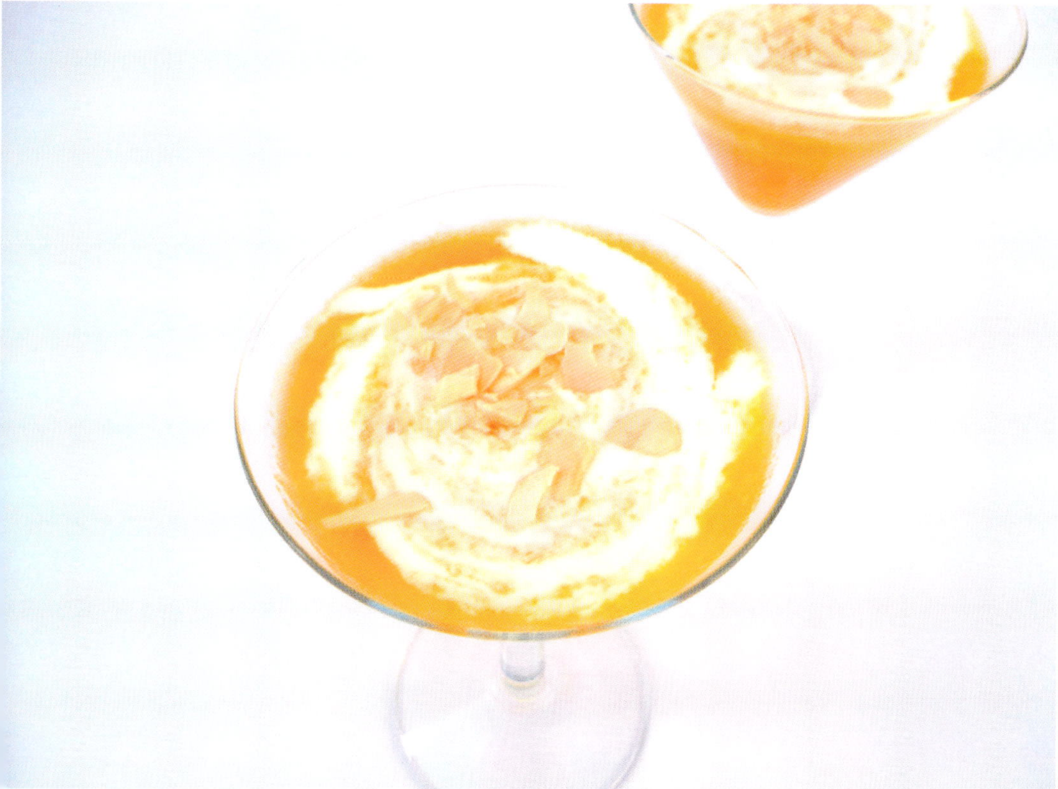

## Simple Caramel Sauce

**Ingredients:**

**115g/4oz caster sugar**
**115/4oz butter**
**2 tablespoons golden syrup**
**1 small tin condensed milk**

**Method:**

Mix all the ingredients together.

Put all the mixture into a saucepan and bring to the boil for 5 minutes, stirring continuously.

Pour over vanilla or coffee muffins.

## Macaroon Biscuit Cream
a change from ice-cream

**Ingredients:**

**260ml double cream**
**2 egg whites**
**1 tablespoon caster sugar**
**3 maracoon biscuits +**
**1 macaroon biscuit for decoration**
**1 tablespoon sherry or other liqueur. My favourite is baileys cream.**

**Method:**

Whisk the double cream until stiff. In another bowl whisk the egg whites, add the sugar and continue to whisk until soft peaks. Put the macaroon biscuits in a plastic bag and crush into crumbs using a rolling-pin.

Add the sherry or other liqueur to the cream and fold in the stiff egg whites then add the macaroon crumbs.

Spoon into individual glasses and chill in the fridge.

Sprinkle with the crumbs of the fourth macaroon biscuit before serving.

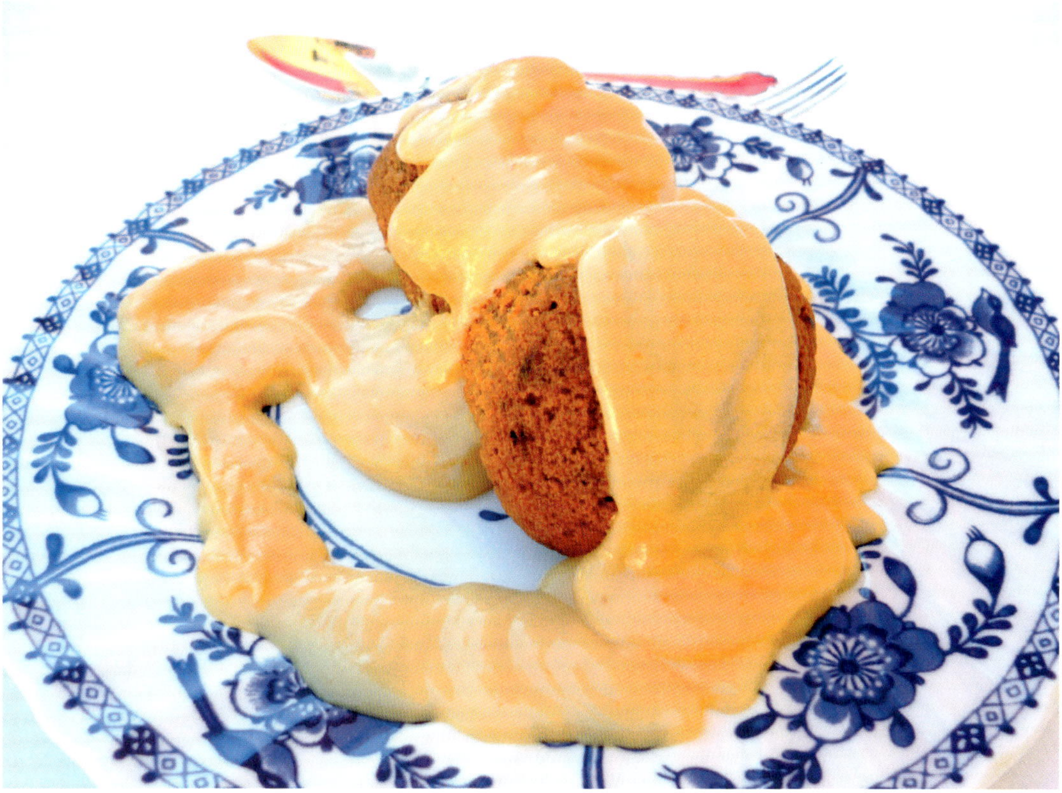

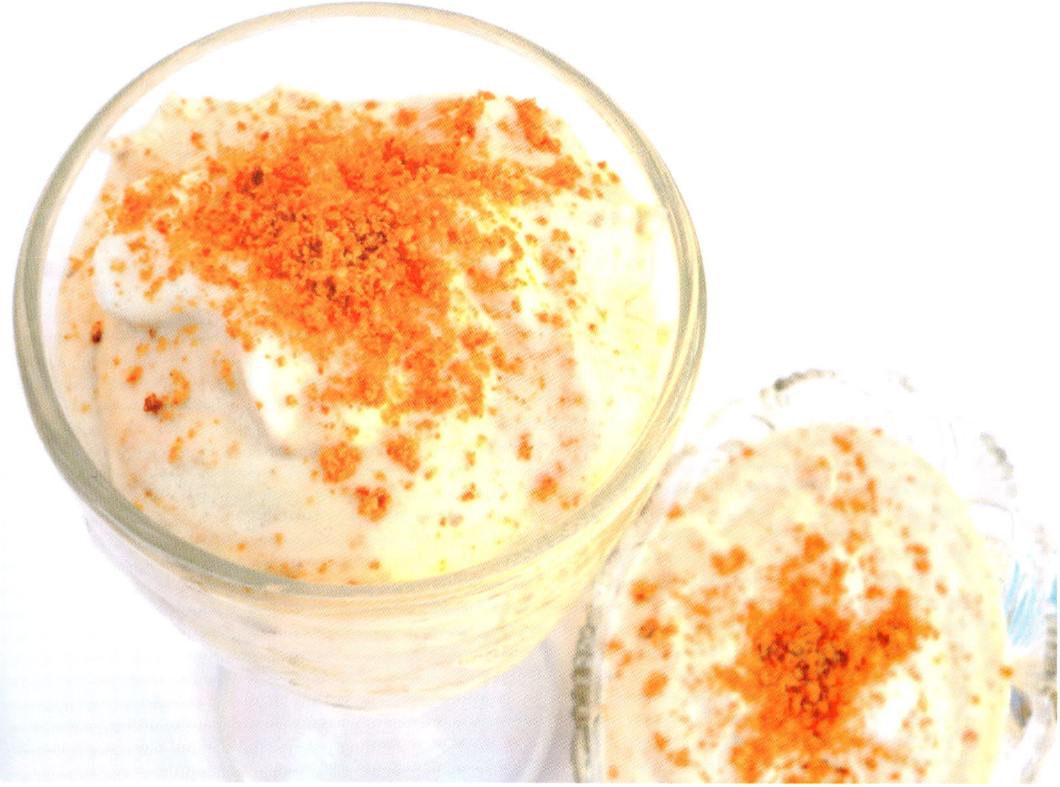

# Index

| | | | |
|---|---|---|---|
| Amaretto Sauce | 92 | General Tartar Sauce | 30 |
| An Oriental Sauce | 58 | Garlic and Chilli Cream | 82 |
| Apple Sauce | 50 | Garlic and Sherry Vinegar Dressing | 10 |
| Apricot Whipped Mousse | 106 | Grand Marnier Cream | 100 |
| A Simple Tomato Sauce | 56 | Granola Topping | 102 |
| A Spanish Sauce | 66 | | |
| Asparagus Sauce | 74 | Herb Butter | 56 |
| Avocado Sauce | 38 | Herb Butter Sauce | 40 |
| | | Herb and Celery Light Dressing | 4 |
| Balsamic and Garlic Dressing | 16 | Herb Salad with Lemon Oil Dressing | 4 |
| Banana Ice Cream | 106 | | |
| Barbecue Chicken Marinade | 80 | Highland Cream Sauce | 104 |
| Barbecue Sauce | 62 | Hollandaise Sauce | 28 |
| Basil and Balsamic Creamy Dressing | 2 | Homemade Bread Sauce | 72 |
| Brandy Butter, (Whipped) | 102 | Homemade Horseradish Sauce | 54 |
| Brandy Sauce | 94 | Homemade Mayonnaise | 12 |
| Bread Sauce, (Homemade) | 72 | Homemade Mornay Sauce | 36 |
| Butterscotch Sauce | 96 | Homemade Parsley Sauce | 34 |
| | | Homemade Tomato Sauce | 48 |
| Calming Rosemary Dressing | 2 | Homemade White Sauce | 32 |
| Caramel Sauce, (Simple) | 108 | | |
| Cashew and Apple Coleslaw Dressing | 18 | Lemon Sauce | 94 |
| Celery Sauce | 72 | Lentil and Bacon Dressing | 64 |
| Cheese and Onion Sauce, (Rich) | 20 | Lime and Turmeric Mayonnaise | 26 |
| Cherry Sauce | 82 | | |
| Chilli Dipping Sauce | 78 | Macaroon Biscuit Cream | 108 |
| Chocolate Sauce | 98 | Madeira Sauce | 68 |
| Chocolate Sauce, (Creamy) | 92 | Mayonnaise, (Homemade) | 12 |
| Cold Cucumber Sauce | 64 | Mayonnaise Sauce, (Mustard) | 10 |
| Cool Tomato Relish | 60 | Medium Hot Dry Pepper Mix | 46 |
| Creamy Chocolate Sauce | 92 | Medium White Sauce | 68 |
| Creamy Orange Sauce | 78 | Mint Sauce, (Fresh) | 46 |
| Creamy Salad Dressing | 6 | Mixed Fruit Sauce | 84 |
| Creamy White Sauce | 26 | Mixed Spice and Yoghurt Sauce | 86 |
| Cucumber and Yoghurt Mixture | 60 | Morello Cherry Sauce | 74 |
| Cucumber Sauce, (Cold) | 64 | Mornay Sauce, (Homemade) | 36 |
| Curry and Honey Sauce, (Tasty) | 48 | Mother's Salad Cream | 8 |
| Custard Sauce, (Fresh Vanilla) | 100 | Mushroom and Yoghurt Sauce | 54 |
| | | Mustard and Garlic Dressing | 34 |
| Dressing for Salmon | 38 | Mustard and Lemon Sauce | 36 |
| | | Mustard Mayonnaise Sauce | 10 |
| Egg and Sweet Almond Oil Dressing | 6 | | |
| | | Olive Oil Dressing | 8 |
| Fresh Mint Sauce | 46 | Orange Marinade, (Sweet) | 84 |
| Fresh Vanilla Custard Sauce | 100 | Orange Sauce, (Creamy) | 78 |
| Freshwater Fish Marinade | 24 | Oriental Sauce, (An) | 58 |

| | |
|---|---|
| Parsley Sauce, (Homemade) | 34 |
| Potato and Wine Sauce | 40 |
| | |
| Raspberry and Honey Sauce | 96 |
| Redcurrant and Ginger Sauce | 52 |
| Red Wine Marinade | 88 |
| Red Wine Sauce | 86 |
| Rich Cheese and Onion Sauce | 20 |
| Rosemary Dressing, (Calming) | 2 |
| | |
| Salad Cream, (Mother's) | 8 |
| Salad Dressing, (Creamy) | 6 |
| Simple Caramel Sauce | 108 |
| Spanish Sauce, (A) | 66 |
| | |
| Strawberry Sauce | 98 |
| Sweet and Sour Sauce | 50 |
| Sweet Orange Marinade | 84 |
| | |
| Tarragon and Celery Sauce | 24 |
| Tartar Sauce, (General) | 30 |
| Tasty Curry and Honey Sauce | 48 |
| Thyme and Parsley Balls | 76 |
| Thyme and Sour Cream Dressing | 14 |
| Tomato and Coriander Sauce | 32 |
| Tomato and Yoghurt Dressing | 18 |
| Tomato, Basil and Red Onion Side Dressing | 14 |
| Tomato Relish, (Cool) | 60 |
| Tomato Sauce, (A Simple) | 56 |
| Tomato Sauce, (Homemade) | 48 |
| | |
| Walnut and Herb Marinade | 30 |
| Watercress Cream | 16 |
| Whipped Brandy Butter | 102 |
| White Sauce, (Creamy) | 26 |
| White Sauce, (Homemade) | 32 |
| White Sauce, (Medium) | 68 |
| White Wine Cream | 42 |
| | |
| Yoghurt Snow Cream | 104 |
| Yorkshire Pudding Mixture | 66 |

**NOTES:**

**NOTES:**

**NOTES:**

**NOTES:**

**NOTES:**

**NOTES:**

# The Author

Elizabeth Tuddenham is a teacher of English as a foreign language who loves cooking for her family and friends and over the years has discovered that sauces, dressings, creams and mousses are a valuable compliment to food. This is the first recipe book written by Elizabeth and designed to share her ideas with the reader. When cooking with her mother and great aunt she learned to mix ingredients which they had regarded as individual, gained from personal experience and passed from one generation to another.

Elizabeth has also collected many recipe ideas from the various countries she has visited as well as the friends she has made during her travels. Cooking is a good way to enjoy and enhance English conversational skills and when exchanging family sauces and dressing recipes with her adult English learners they have shared their different aspects which have very often been passed down through their families giving this book a more interesting variety of both tastes, ingredients and how to compliment a large number of different foods.